MORE THAN A

Mom

FINDING PURPOSE IN THE EVERYDAY MONOTONY WITHOUT LOSING YOUR YOURSELF OR YOUR SANITY

ASHLEY CARBONATTO

More Than A Mom
Finding Purpose In The Everyday Monotony Without Loosing
Yourself Or Your Sanity

To Blake - This whole journey was a little wilder than we anticipated. I'm not sure whose idea it was to have all of these kids, but I'm thankful we're in it together. Countdown for empty nester years is on. #usagainsttheworld

To Brecken, Brenner, and Brynley – thanks for giving me an entire book's worth of material to write about. For your contribution, you can continue living in our house for free. □

Quick Note:

Thanks for picking up this book - I wrote it for you! For the better part of 10 years, the words on these pages have been my actual lived out reality, but it's taken me honestly about 2.5 years to write. Not because it takes that long to write a book that you then self-publish, but because there was so much doubt surrounding my belief in ME, and the words that I had to share. So, in some of the stories my kids are all different ages, which can be confusing and may seem like I have five more kids than I actually have. But I wanted to keep it as close to the real-life lived experience in order to protect the authenticity of those seasons and moments. It is as authentic of a recall as I could come up with..

I pushed through the self-doubt in getting this into your hands because I kept thinking about you. I kept thinking about me and how I WISH someone would have said these things to me to save me the heartache, tears, and stress I've walked through. Nobody freaking told me being a mom would be this hard! Hell, hardly anyone is really talking about it still today! Thankfully, I've found my people who I know I can text middle finger emoji's to sometimes late at night when it's just been a day, but who know the real me enough to know that I just need a safe space to land. They know the flood of emoji's are not cause for alarm to call CPS; the children will be alright! On the off chance you haven't found your people yet though, and you're feeling on an island as you navigate this whole 21st century mom life – I wanted to be that person for you. The shortcomings, the failures, the swear words out loud or in your head –

they're all welcome here. I know that's not who you are, and I also know that you are doing so much better than you think. Motherhood is freaking hard! And if anyone tells you otherwise, RUN (just kidding, but definitely don't trust them!).

These words and stories that I share with you are 100% true...according to my memory. They are lessons and chapters that I feel like I've earned. But also, that I feel like are universally experienced and felt. These are conversations we're having in the alleyways and crevices of playdates and park meetups. This book is not for the cute mom in the pickup line who is crushing life – I'm happy for her! This book is for the rest of us. The ones barely holding it together on the daily, who are just counting down the hours until it's socially acceptable to climb into bed or pour a glass of wine. For the mamas who ran companies and built teams as a BOSS, but then found themselves suddenly in a 24/7 world submitting daily to tiny bosses that she couldn't control. These words are for the mamas who knew deep down this was a job we wanted so desperately, but when we showed up weren't sure exactly how we were going to fit in. There is no mold for us, and after 10 years I finally stopped trying to shove myself into one like your favorite pair of pre-pregnancy jeans. I've let it go and walked through the forest to find freedom. So if you feel lost in the forest today, let me be your guide to freedom. Sit back, turn on a quick 7 hour show for the kids (or whatever it is that you do to ignore them), and re-discover the woman that you were created to be. Sure, mom is your current title? Yep, check. But friend, I believe that you are so much more   than   a   mom.

More Than A Mom

Finding Purpose in The Everyday Monotony Without Losing Your Sanity or Yourself

By Ashley Carbonatto

Job Description for the Hardest Job Ever

Job Title: Mom. Mama. Mum. Mommy. Mother. Maw. Mumsy. Ma. Female Parent. MOOOOOOMMMM.

Department: Department of Homeland & Household Operations.

Supervisor: None. Technically you will be supervised by no one, yet the reality is that you will have a peanut gallery full of people with opinions on how you should be doing your job. Also, disregard the tiny humans demanding your attention, despite their efforts – you don't actually work for them.

General Job Description: No two days will be alike. In fact, as long as you continue reproducing and adding to your brood, no two children will be alike. Your daily goal will be to survive. Some people might think you should thrive, but let's keep the bar low.

Duties and Responsibilities:

- Director of Social Activities
- Executive Producer of Christmas, Easter, Halloween, Birthday Parties, 4th of July, St. Patrick's Day, Valentine's Day

- Nurse, Doctor, Therapist, Handy (Wo)Man
- PTSA, Art Docent, Field Trip Chaperone, & Class Party Mom
- Maid, Taxi Driver, Homework Supervisor, Chef, Referee

Primary Objectives: Raise kind, generous, productive, independent, responsible, inclusive humans while not screwing it up along the way. Super easy.

Hours Required: The hours for this role will vary, from all of the time to every single waking hour of time. Time off is limited. All major holidays need to be honored and celebrated, but please note you will personallybe in charge of overseeing the production for each event. Refer to Pinterest for each meal, party, and wardrobe selection you are required to make on the daily.

Pay: This is actually an unpaid role, where all of your work will be completed pro-bono. Occasionally, you will receive paper crafts and self-portraits that are meant to resemble you but might look more like a Picasso rendition. These are original pieces of artwork and worth nothing in the marketplace, but they say they are priceless in the eyes of the artist. Time will tell. Stuff them in a box to be assessed *(for the trash)* at a later date.

Benefits: Free muffin top, an ever-changing wardrobe that doesn't fit because your body has changed sizes so many times *(see also: yo-yo body)*. Flexible work hours –

can range from graveyard to daytime shifts, although you don't really get to choose.

Required Knowledge, Skills and Abilities:

- Flexibility. Preferably in the vaginal area *(there are work-arounds for this though)*; but emotional flexibility as well – each day will bring about thousands of variables once the little people begin to walk and talk. Good luck!

- Options in parenting strategies. Just search: Parenting Books at your local library and this will provide you with thousands of options in sleep and parenting strategies from varying experts (whom have never met you or your children). Finding time to read them will have to be after-hours, on your "own" time. *See also:* Attachment, Reattachment, Free Range or Helicopter Parenting.

- Master of answering the same question 100 times.

- Ability to predict meal necessities, and any potential variables that may occur during a given outing. Please always carry a pack of band aids, spare snacks *(for your kids plus other kids)*, outfit changes in multiple sizes, hand sanitizer *(organic preferred)*, sunscreen *(no aerosol)*, spoons, straws, deck of cards for entertainment *(no screens!)*, stickers, diapers, wipes, and socks. Don't forget to leave room for your wallet.

- You will need to purchase a bigger bag for daily life because, well, see above.

Education and Experience:

College degree and age will not affect ability to succeed in this role.

Physical Demands:

- Body stretching
- Sleep deprivation
- Constant bending over
- Willing to be on feet all day
- Sleep deprivation
- Chasing rogue ones out of the street and crosswalks
- Wrangling during public tantrums
- Swim lessons
- Sleep deprivation
- Spontaneous [current] dance moves (Whip and Nae Nae, Flossing, Hype, Twerking and Stanky Leg for example)
- On the job training will be administered for mastering ninja moves to place a sleeping baby

into their bed after they've fallen asleep, or remove oneself from sleeping toddler bed

Physical Work Environment: Lots of flexibility here! Wherever you choose to set up shop for the day (*or the moment)* it will most likely be a disaster, so keep this in mind when choosing furnishings for your space. Avoid white anything. Outside help to maintain cleanliness is suggested but only recommended if 2 hours of a clean space is worth the financial endeavor. In fact, use outside help at your discretion. Or just get a dog. SEE ALSO: *Taylor Swift's This is Why We Can't Have Nice Things* for more insight.

Disclaimer: There is no bonus potential and the path up the ladder is foggy. No options for internal promotion until the last child has graduated. Buyer beware though, some tend to boomerang back home so don't make too many life plans.

If someone would have handed me a job description for motherhood before I had kids, I probably would have declined the role and continued forward in my career. I would have read over the hours, the pay, and the job requirements, laughed and then tossed that beautiful piece of linen paper in the trash (*let's be honest, the job description is more likely to be on construction paper than linen paper; I digress*). After all, I worked in Human Resources from the time I graduated college until I began cranking out children like a regular old baby factory. Reading and writing job descriptions, and hiring the right candidate for each role was exactly what I did.

This was my career! Negotiating salary and time off was a regular part of my daytime duties. I took the job of being a Mom, sight-unseen. I had no idea what my work environment was going to be like, who my supervisor would be, or even what the physical and emotional requirements would entail. I said yes to the hardest job ever without having an actual clue in hell what I was doing. Of course, I'd researched this job extensively. I had watched Three Men and a Baby, Full House, and Look Who's Talking One *and* Two – if they could do it, surely, I could. I'd even picked up a couple babysitter and nanny jobs on my climb up the education ladder *(all of which were perfectly capable of wiping their own butts)*, so surely, I had enough of a foundation to rock this role. I had successfully helped run an HR department for a multi-million-dollar fashion brand at the ripe old age of 23, I had graduated college early and landed the man of my dreams before any of my other friends – so how hard could this baby thing be?

CHAPTER 1

Four-Letter Words

"I never know what to say when people ask what my hobbies are. I MEAN, I'M A MOM. I enjoy trips to the bathroom alone in silence." —moms everywhere

"So what do you do?"

It is the most dreaded question that a full-time mom wants to hear when out in public, meeting someone for the first time.

There I was, standing in the middle of a new crowd, all gussied up *(translation: out of my yoga pants for the day)*, and excited for an evening of adult conversation with no little people to interrupt my every fifth word and thought. Sure, my Spanx were cutting my circulation off, but I had no small tyrants shouting demands at me for a couple of consecutive hours. All I needed was a straw in my drink and toes in the sand, and this might as well have been the Bahamas. Despite my dreamy vacation status in my head, I immediately began spiraling at determining how to answer the question posed to me. Do I tell them what I *really* do all day, like pick up crumbs and wipe butts and pass out timeouts like flyers on the street corner? Or do I give them the glam version of the SAHM life where I'm cranking through Pinterest crafts in between meal prep from my Pioneer Woman cookbook while I'm also ironing my husband's khaki pants for work? *(note: you don't know me yet, but that's a joke...I don't cook or iron, well or craft, so there's that).*

"Oh, I'm a just mom."

Ugh.

The feelings of 'less than' immediately overwhelm me. And even though there is still a smile on my face, my insides have sunk a little bit. Okay, a lotta bit. My shoulders have hunched over and my brain is now immediately in fight or flight mode, looking and jockeying for another opportunity to share with these seemingly important business colleagues of my husband's that I am actually educated, used to have a successful career and actually contributed to my family's financial bottom line at one point. The problem is though, whether I'm ready to face it or not, these former career accomplishments are actually legit from another lifetime ago. My achievements in the workplace are quite stale, so much so that the company in which I accomplished them with is no longer relevant and even in existence – they went bankrupt. I'm hanging my pride and perceived ability on a hook that is as rusty and outdated as Hanson's comeback.

My super fancy night of adulting has immediately morphed into a stage where it feels like there's a glaring spotlight on my lack of career. I'm a modern woman of the 21st Century who stays at home and takes care of her kids. Yet I'm suffocating under the façade of a stereotype that exists from the Leave It To Beaver era and feeling like that's the mold of who, and what, I need to fit into because that's how our culture defines success in this job. Of course no one has *made* me feel this way, but it is deeply-rooted in my feelings of jealousy and lack of worth when I hear others talk about the relevant things of today and the world, and the latest deal they are working on. The most exciting thing in my week is that the littlest didn't pee her pants...yet. I entered the evening with great excitement and anticipation, and within 10 minutes of finally escaping the asylum of home, I send myself into a spiral of self-misery. And I'm now immediately longing for those blessed yoga pants to hug my cellulite-ridden thighs while I cuddle up in my usual spot, in the corner of my couch at home, remote in hand, with big decisions to make – should it be Sisters Wives tonight or Teen Mom?

I've been in the motherhood game now for nearly a decade. My career where I collected a paycheck, wore heels, and spent my lunches schmoozing with various colleagues is but a distant memory. Yet for some reason, my gut check reaction when asked what it is that I do is to either downplay my current role in staying home to raise our three kids fulltime, or to boast about a job that I once had, in order to appear relevant and important. My days are filled with anything but fancy-ness. There are no bacon-wrapped scallops being served at our table. It's more like scraps of Peanut Butter & Jelly (*scratch that – we just found out one of them is allergic to peanuts and wheat*), and maybe a handful of grapes and crackers as I hurry through to naptime in order to hopefully get a hot second of quiet in the house to myself.

Just a mom. .The worst four-letter word: *just.*

I had no idea this job would be so hard. I had no idea this job would not be very celebrated in an accelerating world of women's rights in the workplace and advancements in a woman's need and ability to be a contributing member to her family's bottom line. I thought, especially as a Christian, that being a mom would bring about a deep sense of satisfaction. Sure, I wasn't collecting a paycheck anymore, but I could handle the corporate world with ease, so this wouldn't be much different. My days would have reams of flexibility and I could be the anchor for home base so that when my husband arrived at the door each evening, we'd have a peace-filled environment. I'd run things at home, and he'd bring home the bacon, roles that we thought we were both best suited for, despite my girl-power vibes and power couple dreams – at least for a season.

And then we started cranking out babies.

The ease in which I assumed I'd be able to tackle the world of motherhood never came. It was, and is, freaking hard. Like way harder than anything I had ever put my mind to or signed up for. I (*wrongfully*) assumed that I would strong arm, achieve, and dominate this motherhood thing in the same manner that I had managed my way through high-school Spanish: little bit of studying and a lot of flashcards. What I didn't realize though was that I was going to have to go way deeper in my own self-reflection than I had ever gone before; I was going to have to tear back the layers of achievement and accomplishment that I had added to my coat as if it were a letterman's jacket, and really search my soul to find who I really was – just to get through an ordinary day raising three kids.

The messages I received around me were very clear on how women should progress. Culture told me to have kids. The media said this is what women do. It would be fun they said. Well, clearly whoever the proverbial 'they' was, hadn't raised kids in the Gen-X/Millennial era. Motherhood today is something that we have never seen before. We are bombarded with social media pressures, highlight reels of our friends, and our virtual friends, and we are all attempting to raise children who are not entitled and self-consumed. This is unprecedented territory for us, and frankly, being a consumer in our social media culture has led me down a quick path of comparison and feeling completely unqualified and unworthy of the job that I've been given. And chosen. Gone are those precious moments of overwhelming joy and feeling like your heart is going to burst when they placed that precious newborn in your arms. Gone are even the sleepless nights that you thought you'd never make it through (*just kidding – I'm convinced those don't actually end*). Once all of the initial joy wears off, the meals from your friends stop flowing in, and you've experienced your first diaper blowout in public, you find yourself in the trenches of parenting. In the throes of motherhood, I was left feeling overwhelmed that they have in fact chosen the wrong gal for the job, and I'd please like a one-way ticket back to anywhere but here. These kids? Yep, I birthed them, I chose them, they came at my request. But I've had a good run and now I'd like to retire and try something else. Like maybe go back to those bacon-wrapped scallops in the corporate world. The manual on how to raise these minions hasn't showed up in the mail yet, and as far as I can tell, everyone around me is CRUSHING it. And me? Well, I'm struggling at best.

Except crushing it is relative, and definitely not a clear picture of reality.

As I have begun to dig deeper, I have learned a few core truths about what's *really* happening behind those cute little squares and news feeds we scroll on the daily. There are no shortcuts to raising kids. There are no hacks that will give you instant success, no matter how desperate you try. There is no parenting method, sleep training technique, or Super Nanny-ism that will bring about the feelings of satisfaction and worth that we crave as moms. No amount of crustless dolphin-shaped sandwiches will guarantee a happy childhood and no amount of happy hours will bring about the fulfillment you desire your life to have *(although I've tried A LOT of these, and while they won't bring about lasting contentment or purpose, they do play a different role which we'll cover later, so don't worry)*. Motherhood, to my knowledge at this point, is the hardest job ever.

The only way through this thing, is through it. We learn as we go. And if we're wise, we can apply the lessons that others have learned alongside, or ahead of us, to help lay the bricks of our journey. But none of it will guarantee a paved path or road of ease. Raising kids is HARD. It is long. It is gut-wrenching and wonderful all at the same time. Nothing has ever pulled, tested, or made me scream or cry more than being a mom. And yet, I still show up day in and day out for these kids. Because at the end of the day, when they are all tucked into bed, my heart swells. I do love them; I swear I do. If you're a mom, you understand this at your core. How can we love something so much that also drives us to borderline levels of clinically crazy?

The more that I talk about this with other moms, the more that I have come to understand a more universal truth about moms: we are all in the same boat. None of us know what the hell we're doing, and frankly, if they're being honest, none of the generations of women who have gone before us knew either. And we all turned out *(debatably)* fine. There is a common thread amongst moms of today; we all have similar aspirations and goals for who our children grow up to be. We want to raise kind, grateful kids who love well and feel purpose and significance in who they are. The tension comes though when as moms, we don't feel or experience those things for ourselves. We have bought into the lie that being a good mom means dying to ourselves day in and day out until one day you wake up and you don't even know what brings you joy outside of your kids anymore. The title of mom feels all-consuming. But I believe that motherhood does not have to mean martyrdom. We can have a strong sense of self, and pursue our own dreams and passions, in TANDEM with raising our kids. We just need to set out with a vision of who we want to be in the midst of motherhood, which is much easier said than done – I know this firsthand. Culture will tell us that this season will go so fast, so don't blink or you'll miss it. So we get really caught up and worried about missing it, and oftentimes we miss *ourselves* in the process. Who we are becoming becomes a secondary pursuit to us raising our kids and ensuring that these little people become who they were made to be. Except in that pursuit, we neglect who WE were made to be! The path from one mom raising her kids, to the next mom raising hers is vastly different. So, there's no formula or methodology that is going to bring about the sense of purpose and certainty in raising kids that we are all looking for. In a nutshell, our identity is what gets called into question. Are we just a mom now? Is this all there is?

This is the story of the beginnings of my motherhood journey. My hope is that by sharing my struggles, my dark days, and how I've battled back to re-discover confidence in who I am outside of only motherhood, that you will feel a little less alone and a sense of solidarity in the fact that we are all in this together. We need each other as women, and we need to be cheering one another on. That as a mom, tasked with raising the next generation, it is a big job. Probably one of the biggest you'll ever be tasked with. But it is not *all* there is for you! This title of Mom is not your end-all be all, despite how demanding these little people are right now. There are so many variables, so many nuances, and so many forks in the road that if you let it, will leave you feeling exhausted, beat up and wondering if this is even worth it.

But I have to believe it is worth it. Raising kids is the means in which we move the human race forward. That *has* to be a worthy means to spend our time and life. This thing called motherhood is so meaningful, significant, and worthwhile despite the daily monotony required to get the job done. Oh, the daily monotony! Most days of mom life feel like a scene straight from Bill Murray's *Groundhog's Day,* except there is no Hollywood ending *(that I know of yet)*. And yet it is through this everyday grind, of showing up for the job that we have placed in front of us, that we begin to uncover an identity for ourselves that is so much more more than a vocation. Some of us have chosen this role, some prayed for it, and some have not. Regardless of how we each got our current title, we have the opportunity to influence and change a generation

15

through our work at home. And yes, I fully believe this is WORK. Moms are so needed, and as far as I can see, they aren't going anywhere unless cloning really takes off, which with Elon Musk at the helm, maybe might just happen. But for now, we are not a generation of quitters, and we're not going to start now with our kids, or ourselves. So, we're going to need to tackle what's holding us back, head-on, in order to fully step in to our potential to become and re-discover exactly who we were made to be. Strip down the expectations from TV land's great moms, strip down your mother's ideal or example she set *(or didn't set)* for you, and really discover who you were created to be and why you are the exact right girl for this job, for these kids.

This is less of a parenting book and more of a mom book. What's the difference you ask? For starters, I'm not a parenting expert. Ha! I'm the farthest thing from it. I hold no formal pedigree in child-rearing and no psychology degree in Childhood Development. Nope. I do hold a degree from the School of Hard Knocks though – being out in the (suburban) streets raising kids for the better part of a decade *(I actually do have a college degree that is completely and utterly UNDER-utilized in the vocation of motherhood...thanks Mom & Dad!)* This is rather a book for moms. From a mom, to a mom. Girlfriend to girlfriend. I want you to learn and hear all of the things that I need to learn and hear every day. I'm writing this book as much for you, as for me. No one is standing on a pedestal, or at a desk, or in a meeting, giving you praise and affirmation every day.

When we don't hear it, the story that we start telling ourselves, starts to become one of negativity and doubt, and that needs to change. If you're anything like me, you probably just lack the tools to help you combat those lies that your negative narrative coaches you to believe. The truth of the matter is that you are doing better than you think. You have purpose and significance "just" in the task of raising kids. This is important work. You are MORE than a mom. We have the opportunity to shape the next generation. And it starts with us. It starts with how we look at the world and view ourselves. That lens will be the exact lens that gets passed down.

As a generation of educated women raising up the next generation, I dream that we can breed confidence, not cockiness. Let's breed purpose and significance, not generational oppression. If you feel like you are not equipped for this task, sister, keep turning the page and hear me out as I share with you why you ARE equipped. You are up for this job, with what you have right now. Sure, you might need a few more tools in your toolbox – but those things are easy to add. We can work through that. Whether your kids are able-bodied, special needs, on the spectrum, leaders, followers, introverts or extroverts, biologically yours or chosen by you, YOU are meant to be their mom. You have everything you need to do it well. But it's going to start with digging deep from within to muster up the strength and courage to continue showing up, even when you mess up or don't feel like coming to work for the day.

There are no sick days and no vacation days. Maybe if you're lucky, you'll get a meal break. Otherwise, it's game on.

Maybe you have picked up this book because someone recommended it, or you liked the cover, and now you find yourself in a place where you have 2.5 kids, have been at this mom thing for a good chunk of time, and are finding less and less of the "who" you thought you were in your everyday life. Your days consist of activities and chores that are mind-numbingly monotonous and you're struggling to even remember who you were, who you *are*, outside of the title of Mom. Maybe you've even had the thought that there isn't anything left for you outside of motherhood. Gosh, maybe that thought even excites you! If that's the case, this probably isn't the book for you. I'm not your girl and that hasn't been my journey. But if you find yourself floundering on the daily, wondering if this is all there is left of you? Crumbs and naptimes and playdates with half-finished sentences and thoughts, and you feel like you might poke your eyes out if one more kid yells MOM, then this IS the book for you! I feel like you should know though that I'm not an expert, and I haven't arrived. Whoops – wrong book if you thought I knew what I was doing or talking about it when it comes to parenting these terdburgers we've chosen to raise. But there are some tools that I've picked up along the way, and some MAJOR fails, that I think by sharing with you will at minimum, help you feel less alone, and best-case scenario encourage and inspire you to keep going.

The days are looonnnngggg, but the years are short (*they say*), so buckle up mamas, we've got quite the drive ahead   of   us.

CHAPTER 2

Surviving Not Thriving

You should know right out of the gates that I am a 3 on the Enneagram. For those that aren't familiar, this personality type is most commonly referred to as "The Achiever". This is not the book on how to discover yourself through the Enneagram, there are much more versed people in this field (*see my resource guide at the end of the book – all of the experts are listed there!*). The Enneagram Institute describes a type three as:

> *The success-oriented, pragmatic type: Adaptive, Excelling, Driven, and Image-Conscious.*[1]

Driven, Excelling, Image-Conscious – check, check and check. Basically, I was born and bred to be

---

[1] The Enneagram Institute:
www.enneagraminstitute.com

successful because it was simply in my nature. (*insert laughing emoji because, yeah right if only it were that easy...*) What it actually means is that I naturally receive value and worth from achievement. Which maybe will help you to understand why when I found out that I was going to become a mom, something innately in me just assumed that I would kill it.

Now enter motherhood. Being a mom to little people, there are VERY few achievement-oriented accolades to collect on the daily. No paycheck, no report cards, no regular praise. In fact, the real estate that formerly housed my accolades (the fridge) is now overtaken with construction paper creations or certificates celebrating everyone in our house except for me. That may sound trite to some, but truly it's just one of the tiny things that began to unravel me, and my sense of identity as I went through each of my days. When you choose to become a mom, you're signing up for long hours, very little pay (*just kidding, you get zero pay*), no vacation time and a tiny little dictator that's as cute as a cherub, but as ornery as a caged shelter cat.

Raising kids is like watching grass grow. Slow. Steady. Nothing. I am wired to see results, to achieve in order to ultimately to feel valuable and worthwhile. But my first few (*let's be honest, several*) years of being a full-time mom at home preyed on my basic fear: that I was worthless. I had nothing left to contribute and all of the things that I had worked my entire life toward had now been reduced to spending my hours picking up crumbs and plugging myself into the wall to be milked like a dairy factory. My wardrobe consisted of baggy college sweats that were now covered in copious amounts of spit up, slobber, and snot. And those fancy high heels that I used to literally RUN in through the hallways of my corporate job were collecting dust at a rate that I didn't care to acknowledge.

My career was gone, along with the regular praise and admiration from the world. And I was left with these tiny dictators that I had created. Well, technically *we* had created them, but from the hours of 9-5 (*and beyond)* there didn't seem to be much of a "we" helping navigate these new waters of baby "bliss". Someone send help stat.

Enter the go-getter catch-phrase of today's best self-help gurus: thriving not surviving. Every time I would hear it from another mom with seemingly perfect beach waves in her hair and a butt tighter than Cameron Diaz, I would just roll my eyes. Seriously Instagram lady? We are not thriving over here! You try tube feeding this baby on zero hours of sleep and then come talk to me about thriving. You try juggling two toddlers and an infant, just praying that nap o'clock will line up today so that maybe, just maybe, you might get a chance to hop in the shower. I'm not even asking to wash my hair, I'm just talking like quick rinse cycle, barely in there long enough to get a lather of soap on your lady parts. Mama just needs five minutes. I never knew motherhood would demand this much from me. I just literally had zero clues.

It was the start of my thirty-first year, I had a 4-year-old, a 2-year-old and a newborn who was a five-pound preemie and currently living in the NICU. The insides of my body felt like they were falling out on the daily, and my life consisted of a nurse waking me up every 3 hours, usually in a cold sweat, in order to pump. I was three kids deep and more lost and lonelier than I had ever been. There were visitors in those first few days in the hospital, but you know how it goes, three kids, people sort of assume you got this. Which honestly, was exactly what *we assumed* would be our reality too. But in actuality, I had no freaking clue what I was doing and I was more overwhelmed at the thought of bringing this little baby home who couldn't breathe, eat, or maintain her body temperature on her own, than ever. I was quickly spiraling. My body was falling apart but there was no time to tend to that *(we'll just do surgery later to correct that...with a newborn!)*, I had a precious little infant to care for plus the two wild ones at home. My husband was working a job that required over 40 hours a week plus a lengthy daily commute, and I was staring down an everyday life that was mostly reliant upon me showing up to care for them. Zero family nearby and limited pennies to outsource help. Thriving? Yeah, I'm nowhere near thriving. This was PURE survival mode.

And the truth really is that I had already been in survival mode for a while. My pregnancies were anything but a walk in the park, and I regularly joked that it's a good thing I was choosing to have babies in the 21st century with the help of modern medicine, because otherwise I would have been naturally selected right on out. Not sure my body ever wanted to have babies. But my heart did, and honestly, I really thought that would be enough. I had a condition in pregnancy called Cholestasis of Pregnancy, and the only "cure" for it was to birth the baby. The risks were stillborn, and the symptoms were INSANE itchiness all over. I later would come to recognize this condition, and enduring it three times, as a traumatic event and one that definitely triggered major anxiety in me. But in the midst of it, I wasn't processing anything, I was just surviving. I didn't know any better and frankly, what choice did I have?

I truly thought motherhood would be this thing that I would *naturally* just settle right into with ease because obviously I was going to be the best mom ever. It never occurred to me to factor in health issues, strong wills, or strains on my marriage. An equation that I never solved for was that these tiny humans, unbeknownst to them, were attempting to strip me of every piece of sanity, identity, and have-it-all-togetherness I ever thought I had possessed. Little by little, with each passing day of the same routine and same expectations of little people needing every ounce of me, I was losing myself. As a thirty-one-year-old stay at home mom of three, I had no freaking clue who I was anymore outside of MOM.

To the outside world, most would assume that I'm doing quite well and that I've achieved the standard of what some would say is *"Living the Dream"*. I am a thirty-something mom of three, married to my college sweetheart and we have seemingly the most perfect life.

25

I have a well-curated Instagram feed, and all of the yahoos I have come in contact with throughout my life, better known as my Facebook friends, scroll through on the daily to see smiles and health and overall provision by every standard America holds dear. And frankly, using culture's standards as the measuring stick, I *am* living the dream! Cute house, nice neighborhood, good looking kids – the whole package. Yet, over the past eight years, since choosing to formally leave my career as a Recruiter in order to stay home fulltime and raise our kids, I have been plagued with deep-rooted feelings of doubt and worthlessness. Add in feelings of guilt, shame, anxiety, depression – things that I figured were all reserved for seasons of tragedy and seasons of want – and I was a hot mess. I thought these were supposed to be the happiest years of my life. Clearly, I was doing something wrong?

Prior to having kids, my life had been marked with roles of leadership, strength, and abundance. Running departments for multi-million-dollar companies, living the fast-life in Los Angeles and working toward financial goals of home ownership and increased net worth. These were the things that I went to college to achieve! This is why I had spent so many hours working to get good grades and be the best – the payoff was now! But all of that came to a screeching halt when that biological clock of mine started not just ticking, but I felt like, yelling at me, to begin the process of growing our family. All of a sudden everything that I had worked toward, and for, in life was starting to take a serious left-hand turn in the name of motherhood. And because this milestone is celebrated as a giant blessing *(because it is, truly I do believe this)* I wasn't prepared for the underbelly reality that would come my way when I chose to trade in the high heels for burp rags and nap times. I had been raised by two hard-working parents, both of which worked corporate jobs fulltime my entire childhood. I was the product of daycare *(yep, lice)* and overnight summer camps because my parents were always committed to providing a great life for our family. My assumption was that I would just follow in their path, specifically my mom's path, and work full time outside of the home, while raising kids. She did it, so I of course would. I was wired to work. I believed this at my core.

My career as a recruiter was super fulfilling for me. And I was good at it. The pull toward motherhood was stronger though. Slowly, I began phasing out – even just emotionally. We had been married for four years, it felt like "the plan" said kids were next. To be honest, I'm not even sure now in hindsight whether I was super committed to beginning my motherhood journey *in that moment* or if I was just following a path that I thought was *supposed* to be in front of me. Regardless, my career began moving from corporate office boss to flexible work-from-home status as I really started to evaluate stress levels and my ability to get pregnant. Suddenly, my fancy career and climbing to the top wasn't as important. I wish someone would have told me I could do both well *(be a mom and keep my career)*, but alas no sense in wishing things for the past. My job was demanding and my body needed less stress. So I began transitioning to a job and career that was more flexible and would fit a family schedule a little better without having to sacrifice my mental health so much. I took a giant pay cut and began working for our church, running a portion of the kid's ministry. Ha! Me! Running a department centered around kids? I didn't know anything about kids! I was so far over my head, but the job provided an environment that would allow me to put family first. And before you know it, within a month's time of working for the church, I was pregnant.

I think every mom remembers the first time you take a positive pregnancy test. We had been "trying" to get pregnant for many months and I had taken many pregnancy tests prior that all were negative. Each month, my body and heart began to expect to see 'negative'. Lunch break drug store bathroom stalls became my new spot for awaiting one of the biggest verdicts of my life. So when those two lines showed up, I nearly peed. Oh wait, no, I had just done that. My heart stopped. A *positive* test?! There was human life inside me. Naturally, I had to take a second test because disbelief runs rampant when you Google "How frequently do you get a false positive pregnancy test" and yet again, two pink lines showed up. My first call was to Blake of course, followed by my boss. This was insane – I was really pregnant! I was going to be a mom!

Pregnancy was a dousey for me *(we'll get to more of that later)*, and the emotional and physical needs to care

28

for not just me, but this little human both in my body and then eventually out, started to take a serious hold on me. I worked in the margins of my days. There are several pictures of me holding a sleeping infant in one hand, and typing on my laptop in the other just juggling and pivoting all day everyday. It was fun, yet exhausting, all at the same time. When we added the second baby though, things really started to spiral. A major breakdown was occurring where home and these babies were needing me more and more, and my work life was suffering. I hated dropping the balls and letting people down. I spiraled slowly until one day I woke up and realized I hated my job and hated my life. Yikes. Not exactly what your spouse wants to hear. A change was needed. It had nothing to do with my circumstances, or him for that matter, or even the sweet children we had been blessed with. It had everything to do with the lies that I had allowed myself to believe since taking on the title of Mom. My identity was rooted in the achievements and corporate prowess (and potential) I had showcased most of my adult life. I had been groomed to believe that satisfaction would come with ultimate achievement, and I had bought into that lie hook, line, and sinker. I had allowed the slow and subtle lies of the world to creep in and disciple me into believing that my job, my role in my family, was ultimately not good enough, not important enough and not valuable enough because there was no paycheck attached to it and no outside-endorsed accolades. I was failing. Miserably.

Many people in my life I think will be surprised to read that I have struggled with such deep insecurity for so long, because my natural personality is one of confidence and leadership. It's been a front honestly. Well partially at least. A fake-it-til-you-make it effort because really my internal monologue was filled with doubt and shame as I wrestled once I transitioned out of the work-outside-of-the-home world into my role as a full-time mom. The tension of who I was – confident, hard-working, achievement-oriented, successful – paired with my deep-rooted feelings of smallness, not enough-ness, and lack of contentment and purpose were constantly at war in my brain and soul.

I am not enough.

This is all there is for me.

I feel stuck.

For years, I have tried to claw my way back to the surface of that confident girl I once was, the one whom I knew deep down was still inside me. It has felt like something brewing inside of me, as I would try and battle back out of the "mental funk". My pursuit toward purpose took shape of an outlet or vocation every time. Nothing took off though. Or I'd regularly quit before it really could. Social media would call these outlets "side hustles" and I pursued those hard core for many years because through square pictures it seemed to be bringing about purpose for lots of other women and I figured that if I could just create something, make something, start something, THEN I would finally re-emerge. I'd scroll through Instagram or Facebook and see yet another friend building a business that "clearly" was bringing her happiness outside of the home. So I figured I'd follow suit. She probably knows the path better than me.

I started a blog. I stopped the blog. I started painting furniture. I quit painting furniture. I pursued interior design a la Chip and Joanna Gaines, and that didn't take off either. I was pursuing every outlet and expecting success based on ONE TRY. And then when the results weren't coming, I was using that as evidence to prove that I really was a failure. I really did suck. A self-fulfilling prophecy of sorts to reinforce the story I was telling myself that motherhood must be all there was for me. You might be thinking right now that ultimately if I was supposed to write a book, why was I pursuing these alternative avenues? The answer was because I thought that's honestly what I was supposed to be doing. That it was just a matter of finding my "thing" and surely, once I found it I would feel content and happy again. With each step though, and each perceived failure of a business venture, I would find myself back at the same dead end. I was searching for and measuring each venture using the yardstick of "success" (*I was measuring myself against Chip and Joanna Gaines – I mean, in hindsight, what the hell was I thinking?!*). And I was defining that success by looking to the left and right to see and compare how I was to my peers. All I had to show for all the tireless striving were feelings of emptiness, dissatisfaction, and stagnancy. I spent many hours crying on the phone to my best friend *(one of the few that were let fully in to this struggle of mine...or at least the true depths of it)*, just wondering why I felt like I had SO much to offer and no means to pursue it. And I mean that in a very American way of defining "pursue". There had to be more. More than the monotony of everyday life of being a mom that I was experiencing every single day.

And there was. And there is. It just, in true first-born fashion, has taken me my own path of nearly 10 years of guess and check to figure that out for myself. My worth and identity were never going to be affirmed in anything I *did*. Every bit of what mattered was simply *who* I was. I was wasting time and efforts pouring myself into all these side hustles, while missing the big thing in front of me: *my family*. And me!

I kept hoping that some bigger, better, shinier opportunity was going to soar in and fulfill me. I never wanted to abandon my family, but rather be pulled into something fancier, of bigger prestige, than being "just a mom". Ugh, it makes me cringe even when I hear it now. Just a mom. Looking at how I put myself down for so many years. How I allowed the world to define who I was and the value of the role that I was playing.

The lie that I believed was that success, big or small, was going to bring me a sense of purpose and confidence in the job that I was already doing. I've learned the hard way though that nothing I ever did was going to measure up. That I needed to stop striving and reaching and

32

hoping to achieve. That I was significant right where I was at. Raising the next generation. There is prestige in that. And if the world won't tell you that it's true, let me be the first to tell you it's so very true. You are doing better than you think. And let me tell you why.

CHAPTER 3

The Career Ship Sails

When we got married at the ripe old age of 22, one of the conversations we had during our premarital counseling was what our desired, and expected, roles would be after we began having kids. These are really cute conversations to have because what life experience or real knowledge do you have prior to *actually* being married, let alone at 22 years of age? You basically sit around and dream up situations and scenarios that you *think* will be helpful, but let's be real, no one really knows what's going to go down during pre-marital counseling until they put that baby in your arms and you are months into a constant state of sleep deprivation. Nonetheless, we hashed out what our ideal division of labor would be in our household for an unknown, but planned for, future. I had been raised by two fulltime working parents, my husband by a stay at home mom and working father, and based on my giftings and strengths, I immediately proclaimed that I would most definitely be of the former category. Working career-girl mom. That was for sure in my DNA. We'd be a power couple naturally.

And then I had kids.

Six months after having that first little guy pop out, I began to feel a serious pull between my career and being at home. All throughout my pregnancy, I had fought each of my *(male)* bosses prior to bringing that kiddo into the world for a spot on the team when I returned. My company did not have a formal maternity leave policy *(primarily because we had very few female co-workers and they hadn't needed one up until me)*. I was vastly underrepresented in my workplace, and the tenacious don't-tell-me-what-I'm-going-to-do nature came out every time my bosses would kindly explain to me, "You can totally take time off work. It just will be unpaid, and you might not have a job available for when you come back." These would then escalate into heated conversations *(possibly with tears – ugh, pregnancy hormones killing my power vibe!)*, letting them know I would for sure be back to continue my normal kick-ass pace, I would just need a little bit of time to bond with the little babe. I assured them that I had been raised by a working mom, my spouse was already on board, and I had absolutely zero intention of ever *just* staying home with a baby, or kids, as my actual vocational job.

Famous last words.

The whole quest for a power career was dissipating and I longed to be there for this little cherub more and more. When my heart began to change and I felt the nudge to make a change and retire from full-time working world, I bawled. I bawled because I felt so embarrassed to go back on my word, and my plans, to management. I had fought for my rights to have a seat at the table and worked so hard to prove to them, to me, that I had the grit to do both – I could be a mom and have a career! I felt embarrassed that I was falling into the stereotype of a nice Christian girl, who although educated and highly capable, was now going to be a precious full time homemaker. Whatever that meant. I vividly remember lying in bed next to Blake with tears streaming down my face on the eve of my last day as a full-time work outside of the home mom, wondering if this was *it* for me? That I had peaked at 26, and it was now a downward spiral of spit-up and diapers for me from here on out? That I had worked so hard my entire life, graduated from college early and achieved a fulfilling and successful career, only to subject myself to cleaning up crumbs and scrubbing toilets.

I know it sounds silly in hindsight, to actually articulate that I could've peaked at 26, and I laugh now. But those feelings were so real. It was a serious tension in my heart, and ultimately pride, on whether we as a couple would make the choice for me to stay home full time. It would mean big lifestyle adjustments from an income standpoint – we were no longer dual income no kids, we were one income plus a kid. I now probably needed to take up knitting and homemade baby food recipes because I wasn't collecting a paycheck anymore. I knew deep down that this was definitely a heart choice and one that I felt I had to follow regardless of the outcome, it still just hurt a little.

Now don't get me wrong, I *loved* that first year being home with the little one. He napped so often (*and so well!*), I had newfound freedom to watch delightful shows like Live with Kelly while sipping my morning coffee. I joined several new moms' groups and just dove head first into that world. Playdates, park meet ups, library time, walks – all of the things. Who needs a fancy career – I've got daily dates with Price is Right! It was cute and light-hearted and felt easy. It wasn't until that precious little toddling baby started talking, walking, and oh we began to add more children, that the proverbial shit hit the fan. Peaked? Ha! Oh sister, the fun was just getting started.

Children are a disruption. You know what I'm talking about. Before I even finished typing this sentence, my 5-year-old came in to ask me how many more minutes until dinner. It's 10:00am. Or they're a disruption when you schedule that playdate with the fun new mom you've been wanting to get to know, and you think the kids will get along and play together so well, and you spend two hours together and finish approximately three sentences, and one and a half thoughts. You walk away from the playdate more confused about this friend because you don't know the ending to half of her stories, because ya'll were interrupted so many dang times. Playdates with littles are basically one cliff-hanger of a story after another. I'm pretty sure interruption is pre-programmed into children in order to send moms everywhere into various levels of insanity.

In the same way, motherhood has been what I've come to call, a holy disruption, for me. For a while there, I would've told you it was a disruption, plain and simple, just like all those playdate conversations. But perspective, and years of searching for a vocation that is more glamorous than daily carpool and grocery store runs, has shown me that this role of mothering is actually *the holiest* of disruptions. For anyone that just checked out from that sentence, just hold tight for a minute and hear me out. Motherhood is the place and space that has shoved me, stretched me, and yanked me into my deepest lessons of perseverance and patience. It has shown me the ugliest parts of my character that a career of achievement and success could have never brought out and refined. I experience the deepest levels of loneliness that forces me to step outside of myself long enough to make friends, and cultivate community, the way that I am supposed to. I would never have the levels of empathy for others if I didn't have the holy disruption of motherhood. It wasn't until I realized, and accepted, that motherhood wasn't just this thing along the way – a stepping stone, a necessary box to check off in my LIFELONG TO-DO LIST – but rather *was* the way, that I began to appreciate and find fulfillment in the daily work.

From a young age, we are taught that achievement and success are the way to win praise. Thus, when you're a typical first born like me, you begin to strive for all of the titles and achievements that come your way – team captain, student council leader, honor level this and ASB that. The titles of achievement begin to make up this internal resume of identity for yourself. And all of this is good and fine. Our parents and coaches encourage us with each new achievement and we feel like, *aha this is the way to fulfillment! I'll achieve more and then I feel good about me!* It's what propelled me forward so often, to keep reaching for more and pushing myself to pursue and achieve all of the milestones that I could along the way. Until that holy disruption comes roaring in. And all of a sudden, the praise, the achievements, the report cards, the accolades are gone and non-existent the day you choose to pour yourself full time into motherhood. Nobody is standing there cheering you on, with the carrot of promotion, accomplishment or pay raise to help you measure how good of a job you're doing. And without realizing it, your identity in really subtle ways becomes wrapped up in outside achievement. Except now you're a mom, and that is gone. Here you are, with tiny humans in your hands, having a full-on identity crisis because you don't know how to persevere. You're having to now access intangible parts of you that probably weren't very dominant in the workplace or setting you had prior to motherhood. Sure, as an employee you had to show restraint and leadership and patience in the boardroom and with your co-workers, but now your co-workers at home don't give two effs about your skills and ability outside of getting them a snack. Snack time, NOW! Real patience, and kindness, is now being required in order to really find true inner fulfillment. This is new! And normal that you don't exactly have it perfected yet! The outside world has filled the achievement buckets for you for so long, that you didn't even know that that's where your identity was.

As women, we are set up to fail when we only praise the titles and the achievements. When we ask kids *what* they want to be, instead of *who* they want to become, the emphasis is placed on the title of their vocation rather than the character of their heart. And as someone who was raised in the first generation cutely dubbed "The Trophy Generation", this is sadly the narrative that was inadvertently given to me.

It took a full-on identity crisis after I became a mom for me to begin to unravel the layers of lies I had wrapped my identity around. Goodbye fancy job title. Goodbye lovely paycheck. See ya later client-sponsored lunches. Adios year-end reviews (with bonuses and incentives!). Check ya later corporate Christmas parties and co-worker birthday celebrations. Yep, motherhood disrupts ALL of that. Strips it away simply by placing a teeny tiny human in your arms and saying, *okay, now, go figure this one out.* You've had a road map for how to succeed for everything else, up until now. So...GOOD LUCK!

CHAPTER 4

Never-ending Seasons

Look at the nations and watch. Be utterly amazed. For I am going to do things in your days that you would not believe even if you were told.

-Habakkuk 1:5

If there's any wisdom to gain in parenting, it's that everything truly is a season. I remember so vividly the sleepless nights, the tantrums, the colicky baby who would not stop crying and feeling like, "UGH, what is WRONG with my child?" But if you talk to any veteran parent, they will assuredly tell you with the confidence that only a seasoned veteran could assume, "This is just a season."

Yeah, thank you SHARON. Then, I'm ready for this SEASON to be over. Hashtag, not helpful. But then one day you wake up, and you realize, she doesn't cry when I drop her off at preschool anymore. Remember when he used to yell at me to wipe his butt forty times a day? He doesn't do that anymore. And you have the perspective that aw yes, life really does move on and the hardship that you're currently facing, whether in parenthood or just life, really is a season.

I can choose to then apply this same wisdom to my life, purpose, and career choices. As I sit here and write this, I am on my ninth official year as a full-time stay-at-home-mom, where every single one of those years, I have searched and wondered what my purpose will be.

Every. Single. One. Of those years.

And every time, I end with the same question: "Is this all there is for me?"

The little years? The elementary years? The valley of my marriage? The terrible twos? Having three-nagers run my life? The never-ending carpool and break ups of sibling squabbles from sun up to sun down? I have come to believe that all of it is a season. The key is to see it through. But I've only learned that now the hard way, and with a little bit of perspective. I've learned that by simply *(not easily)* going through. One foot in front of the other. Offering myself grace on days when I don't feel like showing up to work *(which literally means walking downstairs to my kitchen)*. I don't mean that to sound trite and short and non-prescriptive. But it's true – the only way through is...well, through.

Perseverance and endurance aren't uncommon words, but they ARE uncommon characteristics. And in motherhood, the day to day can feel like a marathon that never ends. Except you most likely didn't train for this marathon. You sort of just showed up, filled out the paperwork and got a race number. And now you find yourself running, and running, and running (*cue Forrest Gump commentary...*) And the marathon feels like it's never going to end. How, and why, was this journey of raising kids so unfulfilling and hard for me?

The loudest voice rising above the noise was doubt.

Because doubt for me leads to apathy. And apathy is the exact opposite of perseverance and endurance. One thought will creep in that I'm not good enough, or doing good enough things, and the spiral begins. Before I know it, I'm five episodes deep in Sister Wives because I've told myself that I wasn't good enough in that moment, so I might as well just indulge myself in whatever I want since it doesn't matter anyway.

Oh, apathy is a sneaky one. People rarely talk about it. It's fruits, or lack thereof, sort of just fly under the radar. It is the ugly cousin and rogue sister of laziness, but with a ninja twist. When I was feeling overwhelmed with life, my response when unchecked, was to escape and just retreat. My husband would walk through the door each night, and I'd chuck whichever crying, needy, whiny child needed attention the most and RUN. Sometimes simply to my bedroom or on good days, I'd swing by a girlfriend's house, swipe her up and we would hide together drinking boxed wine in the parking lot of a nearby church (*don't @ me on that one, Jesus always has kept the party going with wine*). Defeated, hopeless, and drowning were all words I could use to describe the hard days. Even still, the sneakiness of doubt creeps in regularly. Just the other night, I found myself curled up in bed at 4:00pm, a babysitter downstairs with the kids, just sobbing. Why did I suck so bad at this job? I am no good for these kids. My husband came to pick me up for date night, I hopped in the car, tears still streaming down my face completely paralyzed and riddled with self-doubt. It's just too hard. It's my fulltime job to raise them, and I'm failing. WAAAHHHHHHHH.

These moments happen to each of us. Yep, even Sharon. It's how we respond to them though that will separate the moms who choose to finish this race with grace, and the ones who can't hack it (*those moms actually end up on Dateline, but that's neither here nor there*).

The antidote to this doubt is simply truth. We need to hear and understand the reality of the situation, but in the moment, deep in the trenches, it's too foggy for us to see and hear on our own. We need our people. We need each other. I need my best friend to remind me that this too shall pass. That I *am* the right mom for that little terd that has gotten a note home from his teacher, and principal, for the third time this week. Motherhood does a number on the ego of someone like me who finds value and worth in performance. When the product of my work (my children) aren't performing in the way that I have taught them, I lose my ever loving mind, and can't help but internalize it. The reality though is that their behavior is not actually reflective of my worth. The two are completely unrelated and cannot affect one another.

Case in point: last night we had some friends over for dinner. We were a couple hours deep into our regular CDP (*Crappy Dinner Party*), and the kids were entertaining themselves with sticks and rocks and all the other imaginative childhood stuff. While enjoying the company of our friends, we noticed a power struggle beginning to ensue amongst the youngest two of the bunch (*which there are six kids between our two families, so if you've ever had friends with kids over for dinner, this is a common thing*). As we sat back and allowed them space to "work it out themselves", the inevitable happened: my kid smacked the other kid right across the face. One of those wind-up hits where everyone gasps.

I immediately got a pit in my stomach. *Are you serious child? We don't hit. If you are frustrated, you may use your words, but hitting is not an option.*

After dealing with the fall out between the 4-year-old and the 3-year-old, all was well and the CDP was back on. And then it happened again – this time tears from two different kids amongst the bunch. So immediately rushing to the crying kid, the story bubbles out amongst tearful sobs that the culprit is again *my kid* (albeit a different of my three this time).

Ugh.

In my head, I'm defending myself immediately: *I SWEAR we have talked about this a hundred million times. I say at least 4,000 times a day that we do not solve our problems with our hands. Hitting is never the solution in our family. When we are frustrated, we have many options of how to express that, but hitting is not one of them.*

I played it cool in the moment, but immediately I'm overwhelmed with embarrassment, shame, and feelings of defeat. My thoughts immediately go to self-preservation mode, wanting to defend myself that I am a good mom, I swear; we do discipline our kids; this is a non-violent family. All of the things. I'm embarrassed that it seems like their impulsiveness in this moment, is a direct reflection on how I'm doing as a mom. That if I was a good mom, my child wouldn't be acting this way, behaving like this, and certainly not hitting other kids. We don't teach that in our family and we certainly don't subscribe to, or show them by example, that hitting is the right solution ever.

Remember our antidote to doubt though is truth. And the truth in this situation is that my value and worth have nothing to do with my kids' behavior. Let me say that louder for the peanut gallery in the back to hear: *Your* value and worth have nothing to do with your kids' behavior! *But what will people think of me? Aren't they judging me? Shouldn't my kids be farther along than this?*

Again, your value and worth have NOTHING to do with your kids' behavior.

So often we wrap our identity up in our accomplishments, our vocations, or our accolades. Or even moreso with our performances. The first things out of our mouths are the things that we are doing right in the world. And this is all good, and worthy of praise, I'm sure of it. But what happens when that is stripped away? What happens when you make a mistake, or in the case of being a mom, when your kids make a mistake? If you have built your identity on the bedrock and foundation of their behavior being good, then sooner or later, the rug will get pulled out from underneath you because your circumstances have nothing to do with your identity or worth.

It is a human desire to know that we are inherently accepted and valued. So usually the only thing we know how to do to check those boxes for our self-esteem is to seek the affirmation for it from the things that we do, or that our children do. But those results are not tied to your identity, your purpose, your value, or your worth. You are SO MUCH MORE than their behavior. And thank the Lord that our value and worth are set in stone. It can't be eroded or lost or moved or stripped away. It just is. A constant in the rollercoaster of motherhood.

You are NOT a bad mom when your child hits.

You are NOT a bad mom when your child throws a tantrum.

You are NOT a bad mom when you get the call from the Principal's office...again.

You are their guide, their teacher and the one to help equip them to make good choices in the world, but their results are not reflective of your value or worth. Sure, they could behave better and we pray they make better choices to impact the world for good, but if we tie our identity and worth to their behavior, we are bound to end up feeling like a failure. Because they *will* fail; we all do.We can combat the self-doubt, insecurities, and ultimately lies that I hear in my internal monologue, by exchanging the thoughts for affirmations and truth. The truth that my kid's behavior is not reflective of me. That I am accepted, secure and significant just as I am. That I have been chosen to raise these kids, but that is not my full identity. That my vocation, and the titles that I own (Mom, Wife, Daughter, Sister) have no bearing on my value as a woman.

So, today, when your kids are fighting, when they are acting a fool – especially in front of others – don't fall trap to the lie that their choices are a reflection of your value and worth. Don't use their behavior as the measuring stick for how you're doing as a mom. Their choices, and behavior, are not your report card.

You are doing a good job mama. Your kids need to be parented, that is your JOB, but it is not WHO you are. Tie yourself to the truths of who you are so that you are anchored to them during the storms of their behavior. I promise you will come out the other side without the anxiety and stress that come along with riding the emotional rollercoaster of their behavior. No way sister, you are not here for their rollercoaster, you are the anchor. And you are worth far more than their best, and worst, days.

CHAPTER 5

One More Lonely Girl

Loneliness is one of the biggest surprises of becoming a mom. I heard NOTHING of feelings of loneliness prior to becoming a mom. But once I dove into this world headfirst, it quickly became one of the loudest voices I battled every day.

You want to know who the lonely are, and what they look like? I bet it's the mom next door. The one that is home, seemingly surrounded by a tiny army that she created herself (well...most likely with the help of *someone)*, confined to an ongoing nap schedule that takes her out of social rotation for a solid two to three hours every day. Throw in snack time and all the meals these children require, and before you know it, you're living in that kingdom of isolation that Elsa all told us to look for. Your day to day is full of isolation.

I would definitely have considered myself a fairly stable person prior to having kids. Now, stable isn't even in my vernacular of adjectives I'd use to describe myself, even on a multiple-choice test of one. The depths of loneliness that I have felt at home during the course of the last eight years raising these kids is simply something that I just never saw coming.

When we added Brenner, our darling second born, he came into our life unexpectedly. And by unexpectedly, I mean on the heels of deep heartbreak. Just before Brecken, our beloved first-born, had his first birthday, we had decided to pull the goalie and began trying to add to our brood. Not dissimilar to how it worked the first go-round, we began our season of intentional "trying" to make said child, and just like my 9th grade Home-Ec teacher told me, one strong swimmer made its way into my uterus. It seriously still blows my mind everytime I sit and think on the actual process of how a baby is created in our bodies and I just can't – my brain explodes every time. Anyway, I wasn't a big ovulation tracker *(primarily because I was too busy at work to track such scientific things)*, but around the time when I figured we could test, I headed to my local drugstore to get a pregnancy test. Which, side note, can we just talk about buying pregnancy tests for a minute? Buying a pregnancy test is TEN TIMES worse, and more embarrassing and nerve wracking than buying tampons ever is or was. Every single time I purchased one, whether at a drugstore or even at the dollar store, I remember standing there feeling so embarrassed and vulnerable that I might as well have just dropped my pants right there in line and peed on the stick in front of everyone. Did anyone else STRESS THE EFF OUT when buying pregnancy tests? Okay, just me. Cool. Moving on.

In that first month, when the pregnancy test came back positive, we were elated! Instead of waiting the suggested three months to share the news with our friends, in typical Ashley live-out loud fashion, we immediately began to shout the news from the mountaintops to all of our people. There was no need to wait – this was a time for celebration! We bought the "I'm Going to be A Big Brother" book and brought it to my parents. We immediately shared with our closest friends without any reservations – yep, Blake had yet another strong swimmer in him and we were crushing this parenthood thing! Our joy couldn't be contained.

But within weeks of that positive pregnancy test, before we had even seen its sweet little heartbeat, I began to bleed. I remember routinely heading to the bathroom without any concern, only to be immediately overwhelmed with shock when I wiped a lot of bright red blood. Panic immediately set in. It was during naptime so Brecken was fast asleep, and I grabbed my phone and immediately called my doctor for re-assurance and help, to which she told me to come in right away for bloodwork. This could be normal, or it could not. Of course, my mom brain immediately goes to the *"it could not"* scenario. In a panic, I immediately dialed a nearby girlfriend who I knew was home too and asked her to come sit at our house while Brecken slept so that I could run to the doctor for some bloodwork because I thought I might be miscarrying. I remember walking into the hospital for my blood draw just feeling numb and hollow. I couldn't look anyone in the eye and my body was just on autopilot. This must be what it felt like for our ancestors in fight or flight – my body was driving and walking and interacting with the phlebotomist, but my mind wasn't there. I was hidden in a shell deep inside hoping that would provide some sort of protection for the heart break that I knew was about to come. By that afternoon, we got the call with our lab results that I was in fact miscarrying. We lost that baby. It felt like the rug had been pulled out from underneath us.

I was devastated.

I didn't understand.

And although I was still in my first trimester, that didn't take away from the fact that we had celebrated and wanted *this* child. It hadn't even crossed my mind that it wouldn't be in the cards. I felt deep grief, and let very few people in on that. I lived in shame feeling like it wasn't a sad enough story to share with people, because I was "only a few weeks along". A lot of people taught me to feel that way too. *"Oh, that's super common to miscarry in your first trimester"*. *"Most women miscarry in their first trimester and they don't even know it!"* As if that irrelevant statistic was supposed to ease the blow of having my dream of close siblings come to fruition.

This was my job. I was a mom. And now, my second baby wasn't going to be mine this side of heaven. I knew this was a "common" experience for women, but it just had never even crossed my mind. Yes, I was still within my first trimester and this happened to women regularly, but I just didn't anticipate that it would happen to *me*. I didn't know the wave of grief it would send over me, and because of that, the subsequent loneliness that would come after. I remember being out grocery shopping with my oldest right after getting my bloodwork done, and then the call, just staring at everyone thinking *if they only knew what I was going through right now*. I was so hurt. I hid in my closet that day and just sobbed. I didn't realize how much I had already attached, had already started to love, and had already counted that little one as part of us; part of me.

I also experienced a second loss during that same season with the death of my paternal grandfather, whom I adored. I remember sitting on his hospice bed in his final days, his cancer had taken over his body and he was a mere shell of his once vibrant self, and letting him know, and admitting out loud for the first time, that I had lost a baby a few months prior, and would he do the honor of hugging that precious child and taking care of it until I could get to heaven? The cancer had taken away his ability to speak anymore, but he sat there and a tear streamed down his face. He knew what I was asking of him, and he knew he was up for the job. It brings me to tears to think about it even now. One of my most beloved people in the whole wide world, getting to heaven and being able to hug my baby and let them know they were loved. He would be the keeper for that little babe until I could get there someday, and that brought me comfort and peace.

If you've ever walked the road of death, miscarriage, or tragedy, you know that there really *isn't* anything anyone can say that is going to help ease your pain. You are going to have to walk that road of grief on your own accord. But people please, for the love, keep the "helpful" (*well meaning, I know*) comments to yourself. God didn't need another angel in heaven. It's so insensitive. Just be there. Just listen. If you aren't sure what to say, then call that out and just sit and be. I remember the three specific friends who in their own way, on their own accord, showed up for me exactly how I needed them to. As themselves, with grieving hearts too. They simply acknowledged the hurt that I felt and that they saw me. I didn't anticipate the level of grief that I felt, and it definitely hurt more when people tried to encouragingly minimize it. They meant well; I know that. But they didn't get it. I know now in hindsight that everyone meant well, but in that moment, I never felt so alone and hurt.

Things for me in my role at home were never the same after those losses. Admittedly, my mental health was probably not the most stable when we decided against doctor's advice, that we would continue to "try" to get pregnant again without allowing my body proper time to heal – both emotionally and physically. I don't normally recommend ignoring the advice of your trusted medical professionals, but for whatever reason we did in that season. Maybe it was the tenacity in me, maybe it was the belief that I just needed to prove I could do this job well, and I didn't allow much time at all for myself to really grieve what had been lost. My heart was treading lightly, and I didn't want to anticipate joy and hope to only have it stripped away again. Because before we knew it, without even another missed period, I had another positive pregnancy test. Our own little rainbow baby entered our lives basically nine months to the date of when our heaven-baby would have. Brenner Joseph (*named after my paternal grandpa*) was a month early and we felt blessed.

CHAPTER 6

Secret Society of Anxiety Meds

Even though we were happy and joy-filled, we traded one thing for the next – or as our premarital counselor had referenced it, we just moved the cheese.[i] Bringing a preemie into our home wasn't the bliss-filled mothering days that I had remembered when we brought our first home. It was there that we found ourselves knee deep in the throes of parenting with a strong-willed toddler, juggling an extremely colicky baby. Nap when they nap, rest as much as possible – well what happens when you have a toddler to juggle and now a preemie that can't be soothed?! Gone were those days of multiple naps during the day, finishing my cup of coffee uninterrupted while it was still hot. This new little one was colicky, fussy and

I could do nothing to soothe him. I began to spiral. I was drowning not only in the daily work of managing two kids, but also just in feeling purposeless and unnoticed in my role. And grief that I never really dealt with. Hello new friend named post-partum!

He cried and cried and cried and cried. I understood shaken baby syndrome, which is TERRIBLE to admit, and even though I would NEVER harm my kids, I began to *understand* how someone would, and *could*, get to their breaking point. Nothing was rational. Everything was hard and everything felt so overwhelming. I was struggling to function and make it through a normal day. Thankfully, we had a village and I went against every bit of advice I had ever been given in order to protect my mental health and asked our friends to keep our baby overnight. Yes, I outsourced my one-month old preemie of a baby for a slumber party. I couldn't do it you guys. I felt desperate. Helpless. I was afraid of my own stress and how little I could do to help this little baby of mine. I knew that I had to sleep, and asking our friends to keep him overnight was the only way that I knew how to not lose my mind. My preemie newborn had his first slumber party at one month old. #okayestmomever

Once I gained some clarity in my brain after that full night's sleep *(minus pumping of course)*, we eventually were able to figure out that our sweet little boy actually had a painful allergy to the protein in dairy and once his diet was corrected, all was well. The problem though was that once his colick had a solution and we were all sleeping, I still didn't totally feel content or purposeful the way that I thought I would. In hindsight, I realize that I sort of just swept all of that experience under the rug and didn't really *deal* with the post-partum, the trauma of a preemie (and subsequent high-risk pregnancy), and the depths of loneliness that I went down to after our miscarriage. By moving on so quickly, and not properly grieving, I figured I could just strong-arm my way through as I had really always done in the past. Grief won't let you do that though. The more you sweep it under the rug, the more sideways those emotions are going to come out in your life. For me, that was in the form of anxiety.

We don't talk about these things as women. They are the ugly parts of motherhood that we want to hide. Keep in a closet. Locked up. Hoping that we'll just power through the season, and it will all go away. This is a lie. Sure, I had told a couple of really close girlfriends that we had lost a baby, but I put up a front that I was totally fine. My story wasn't *that* sad after all because we had a rainbow baby (which is a blessing not everyone gets to experience!) and so I was shamed into tucking those emotions of loneliness and sadness away because everyone told me to be happy and that it's really common to lose babies in the first trimester. Well common or not, my feelings were of sadness. And whether the story is one of great heartache or tragedy or not, there needs to be space for those to be held and processed. We are doing such a disservice to one another when we tell another human what to feel when they are sad, or how to justify it away. It's a natural response, I totally get that, because to sit in the uncomfortable is really freaking hard. And who wants to do that? Not me! Ultimately, that work has to be done on our own. As friends though, we do have a role and I think that we can simply love our people who are hurting in the best ways that we know how and hold space for the sadness, as well as the joy, that they feel. Otherwise, if we don't feel the freedom to feel those things because they're not "sad enough", then we sweep them under the rug and they come out oftentimes in even sadder or unhealthy ways. Brené Brown refers to this as comparative suffering, which is the concept that when we minimize someone's pain because someone else inevitably has it *worse*, we actually make the pain heavier not lighter because there is nowhere then for our pain to go. Our pain becomes not good enough pain. Queen Brené specifically says this:

> *If there's one thing I've learned over the past decade, it's that fear and scarcity immediately trigger comparision, and even pain and hurt are not immune to being assessed and ranked. My husband died and that grief is worse than your grief over an empty nest. I'm not allowed to feel disappointed about being passed over for a promotion when my friend just found out that his wife has cancer...*"[ii]

Our pain is worth our tears and love. As in, there is no such thing as big or little pain – at least when it comes to someone else getting to define it for you. We are the only ones that get to determine the place, value, or rank of our own pain – not someone else. And in fact, when we minimize or compare our pain to others, we actually do ourselves a greater disservice than by simply acknowledging and sitting with the experienced pain. I'm no expert, but it seems like we carry enough in our load of motherhood, that the last thing we need to do is increase our pain.

After we added our third baby, and I experienced my second bout of post-partum, things were at an all-time low in our household and marriage. We were AT each other's throats and every minor fight was basically world war three. And it was terrible. I was my absolute worst self. Yelling, and saying really unthinkable things – usually most frequently directed at Blake. And my kids were definitely not immune from my post-partum wrath either. I was so quick to fly off the handle bars and seemed to possess virtually zero control of my anger and tears equally.

I'm embarrassed to look back at my behavior from that season. But no one was talking about real life that was happening behind closed doors. I wasn't talking about it with them, and they weren't talking about it with me. Even with my very closest friends, the real experience of miscarriage, loss and post-partum wasn't being talked about. And those shoved down emotions were coming out sideways on the daily. Frankly, it's not like an easy light-hearted thing to bring up while you're at a park playdate where every other sentence is interrupted. But also, that is an excuse for a lack of willingness to be vulnerable. To reveal that last 10% of your life with real actual people. This is an issue amongst us women. We let the *fear* of being known block us from actually being known. I know we hear the phrase "no one is perfect" often, and it's almost cliché at this point but it's time that we as a collective group of strong women *start* talking about things. Mental health matters. Your struggles behind closed doors are not exclusive just to you. Bring that crap to the light for goodness sakes. Stop carrying around secrets and shame of your shortcomings, and let's start owning them as catalysts toward becoming better versions of ourselves. The first step starts though by talking about it. I finally asked for help and went to my doctor. She gave me a prescription for a low dose of Xanax.

Anxiety medication was a game changer for me. For the first time in several years, I was able to rationally sort through my feelings on those most stressful of days. My anger was tempered and I was able to regain control of my emotions around the littles. I could have a healthy conversation with my husband even in disagreement without letting my emotions get the best of me. When I shared this with my friends (like a natural influencer does), the responses that I got were blank stares, the look, following by a resounding "me too."

record screeches

Wait, whaattt? I was like guys; I have the key! And they all stared back at me and were like oh yeah, I've been dealing with that for years and also have been taking anti-depressants. Or yep, my doctor just prescribes it immediately after a baby because I go so dark and deep. Even my very best friend, who knew the ugliest parts of me and me of her, hadn't told me that she had been taking medication and dealing with this same struggle for years.

I was floored. Had they been intentionally not telling just me?? Or was this a *thing* that all women hide and pretend like it's not really there? We all have been struggling with these same feelings of despair and loneliness and overwhelm, and no one is talking about it?

It's shame at its best.

Hide it. Keep it tucked away. Pretend like you have it all together. Don't let them in to the last 10%.

Lies. They are all lies.

If we want to be the best moms that we can be, then we need to be talking about the deepest, darkest things, with AT LEAST our closest people. Mental health professionals also highly recommended.

I had no clue that everyone had already been dealing with this, and I was just late to the party - except no one had told me the party even was happening! I just stumbled there by chance.

Actually, not by chance, but by asking for help.

This isn't an official stance or formula on anxiety medication – I am the farthest thing from a doctor, so don't take medical advice from me! But goodness gracious, we have GOT to be talking about this stuff. Our shame keeps us in the dark trenches of suffering, telling us that the problem is *us,* when that couldn't be further from the truth. To think that I had been trying to fix myself on my own strength, on my own accord, almost to the detriment of my marriage, and my friends had an answer all along, in it as well but just hadn't *said* anything, damn near crushed me. We *all* were struggling and NO ONE was talking about it? This all-encompassing struggle that was being kept behind closed doors in everyone's house was perpetuating the problem. Here I was, new mom for the third time on what felt like a total island, comparing my struggles to my neighbors', not seeing her drowning in her every day. She wasn't a crying blubbery mess from sun up to sun down. I didn't see her struggling to get out of bed, or struggling to laugh or feel confident. I was overwhelmed with extreme self-doubt and anxiety wondering why *Karen* had it figured out, but I couldn't get my ish together. Oh wait, Karen was on meds too. Ohhhh...now I get it.

All of us might not need medication to help pull us out of the funk. But we do all need each other. These motherhood days are so long and lonely at times that we can't do it alone. We have to be the generation that makes mental health a non-taboo subject. I can't pretend to know or judge your brain's chemistry or what is best, but I do know that when we hide our struggles out of fear or shame, that not only do we perpetuate our own problems, but we rob our friends of opportunities to feel freedom in their struggles as well. What we hide in the dark grows, but when we bring it to the light, we are set free. I don't care if you need anxiety medication, forty-thousand supplements, an extra glass of wine a night – whatever! The point is not the substance or means for coping or surviving, the point is transparency, authenticity, and vulnerability. We have no reason to fear these things, and yet for some reason we keep these struggles of ours in the dark. In my closest circle of mom friends, we *all* were taking medication to help us in the everyday, but none of us knew it. Which side note, I do realize that I had a role in that too. I need to be the type of friend that leads with love in my relationships and not judgement, even if it is merely perception. Up until that point, I think I had been putting off more of a judgey vibe than I cared to recognize or acknowledge, and thus my friends didn't feel 100% safe with their last ten percent. I was gutted when I realized that, and I committed to doing better. I committed to bringing my struggles into the open air and light because mental health matters, medication or not.

I would say the bulk of my friends now know that I have been on a journey of surviving motherhood with my mental health. They know this because I choose to talk about it out loud. I've done the inner work to excuse the shame right out the door that I would need an extra helper in the shape of a little pill for the time being. My friends know I've taken anti-anxiety medication, and even still we're having these conversations in the quietest places of our hangouts. In the corners of a dinner party, in the car after everyone else has gotten out for the night. I regularly will get late night texts asking which exact medication and what the side effects were and is this a forever diagnosis and how bad it's been at home (*which again, for the record, not an MD*). My heart breaks when I have these chats with my girlfriends, but I also assure them this is not a life sentence or a signal that they are broken or not cut out for this hard job. I'm not even going to get into the amount of hormone psychosis your body goes through from carrying and birthing children, but once you start learning about that, it's no wonder women are struggling with anxiety – the children have done our bodies in! But we do not need to be ashamed of this struggle. We can have freedom in knowing that help is good, and common, and a part of your journey and story, not a signal that you're broken. It will take bravery to bring it into the light and ask for help, but we are more brave than we think and the freedom we receive from total truth of reality will be worth it.

CHAPTER 7
Unfit For The Mold

"I can't even." – Moms everywhere at 5pm

After getting my emotions and hormones more stabilized, I set out on a self-discovery pilgrimage. I switched all of my efforts from parenting and marriage books, blogs and podcasts, to self-help, self-discovery and Enneagram publications. I was beginning to understand that I was going to continue to show up as a partially-functioning parent and wife until I re-learned how to love myself. I needed to find me again. I didn't know where or how to start though.

As I began devouring and peeling back the layers of hurt, loss, and change that motherhood had gifted to me, I began to *remember* who I was. I started to re-see, with new eyes, *who* I was, and frankly, *whose* I was. Before I could take any steps forward, I had to understand and accept that I was first and foremost, a child of God.

Now, for me, I chose to follow Jesus while in high school through a program for teenagers called Young Life. My faith was real and sustained me throughout the years, but the burns of time had led me down a darker path where when I finally began to get my head above water in motherhood, I realized that I had been believing a giant set of lies about my worth and identity for years. I was being held down in bondage and I didn't even know it. I had been holding Jesus at arm's length while simultaneously hoping and expecting him to pluck me from the depths of despair, despite my desires (*and abilities)* to do it on my own.

So I had to start with the basics. This came in the form of general affirmations about my identity and worth.

I am significant.

I am worthy.

I am enough just as I am. Right now, in this moment.

I cannot earn God's love.

I am loved.

I am free.

My focus couldn't be anywhere near the *roles* that I had chosen and been assigned – wife, mom, employee, etc. – I had to start with just me. I've often heard from various counselors throughout the years, including those focused on the study of the Enneagram, that we have to begin thinking about our inner child. The little girl inside you who longed for things from her parents, from the world, from life that did not come to fruition, or was wounded, or hurt, or let down along the way. Now it is my experience that these wounds will come no matter how great or wonderful your upbringing was – ultimately, our people and our spaces will let us down. It is a truth that just *is*, where no one is necessarily at fault (although sometimes they are), it's a reality of living in a broken world. And I had to face down those demons and start there, with my inner child – focusing on her identity and worth. *Who was I before I started to feel overwhelmed as a mom?* What were some of the earliest beliefs about myself that I could remember before the world told me, and taught me, how to behave and feel? When did I stop believing in me? The confident girl voted Most Tenacious in high school, where did she go? And who told her to stop being like that? These were the questions that I needed to start staring down, head on, and sorting through because there was a good chance that there were deep-rooted lies about who I was, and the outside voices I had allowed to write my narrative. It seemed as though I had picked up these lies along the way without even consciously being aware I was digesting them. Their negative narrative had began to weave and grow roots around my soul, making me feel stuck and less than. Lies that had taken up far too much space in my inner being for far too long. Because I wasn't actively, daily, speaking truths about who I am, a crack in my self-worth armor developed and the lies began to seep in. And when you aren't actively speaking truths of affirmation over yourself, practicing them daily, the lies will tell you exactly who you are.

I have a printed card with the affirmations that now sit on my desk in our bedroom that I regularly go to and reference on the days when I feel those sad, dark thoughts creeping in. The affirmations that remind me *who* I am at my core. Everyday titles and hats that I wear get set aside. I was under construction, caution tape and orange cones were out, it was time to pull back the scaffolding and do a full gut job on who motherhood had stripped me of becoming. Now to be clear, motherhood is not the thing that stripped me of my identity and worth. But I had *allowed* it, and more specifically, the world around me, to tell me how I should be acting, how I should be feeling, what I should be doing, and that hadn't ever computed with my natural desires and giftings. My insides didn't match what the outside world was telling me a mom, especially one that stayed at home fulltime, was supposed to look like.

Significant.

Worthy.

Enough.

Loved.

Free.

It is a slow re-build process. Daily. Consistently. Small truths with big impacts over time. The words that we speak over ourselves matter. The truths that we allow in, the voices that we allow in, matter. Once I was able to get my foundation back, I then began to reconcile *why* this job was so hard for me. And it hit me. I am NOT cut out to be a stay at home mom. Or at least the SAHM that I had allowed the world to tell me was expected. I had falsely believed that women who chose to stay at home to raise their kids were artistic, creative, patient, domestic, and just overall really precious. And I believed this because it is all that I saw. I had no model of a kick ass woman out there, who bucked the typical SAHM stereotypes and was a self-admitted domestic underachiever, yet simultaneously still chose to serve in that role for their family for a season.

You can't do what you can't see.

At least that's what I thought.

The SAHM voices were quiet, and virtually non-existent. No wonder I fell into a shame spiral. No one who looked like me was modeling, or encouraging me to keep going. And at minimum, no one that I knew was openly talking about the struggles that they were feeling, which led me to believe a giant lie that I was all alone in my feelings of discontent and stuckness. The stay at home ladies that I knew all had side hustles of creative businesses, Etsy stores, or cute photographing companies. And they were *crushing* it. I tried those, but they weren't me. Something didn't land for some reason. I still felt empty and unfulfilled. They were achieving success (*which was awesome*), but why wasn't I?

So I waited. And I waited, and I waited and I waited. Some days to the point of apathy and laziness. No point in getting dressed in anything but last night's sweats today – it's not like I had anywhere to go other than home. Yay, another day at home. Other days, I'd feel surges of motivation and leap toward a new project, ultimately coming up short yet again. I was chasing after a "thing" to fulfill my identity.

Jennie Allen, in her book <u>Stuck,</u> a study on David from the Bible, speaks to identity when she says, *"the identity we are all chasing has already been given to us by God."* Full stop. Our identity is fixed. Can't be changed, stolen, wiped away, altered, re-written, or stripped away. It has been given to us by God. This was a giant shift in thinking for me because it meant that I had to start reframing how I defined identity for myself. Well who does God say I am? He says: I am a saint. I am blessed. I'm appreciated. I'm reconciled. I'm heard. I'm gifted. I'm loved.

With those truths as the foundation, it was then that I could start identifying who God *had* made me to be, rather than who he *hadn't* made me to be. I began by making a list of all the things that I was, and wasn't. Sometimes, process of elimination helps bring focus around what is true by eliminating what isn't true.

I am not the least bit precious by anyone's definition.

I am a leader.

I can't cook to save my life.

I like to look cute every day, and I'm good at it.

My Pinterest boards are filled with aspirations, but no final projects.

Babysitters are my best friend and I have no problem leaving my children on the regular.

I am a ball-buster by nature.

I've always been a tomboy, and yet I love the luxuries of life.

You are more likely to find me at the hair or nail salon, than you are at the gym.

And if you're looking for me to be the art docent or neighborhood babysitter, ha, think again. I barely like my kids *(most days)*, let alone YOUR kids.

If you've ever seen the movie Bad Moms, you know the SAHM stereotype. Kristen Bell is shown in her everyday life wearing a puffy paint sweatshirt and noodle necklace with her kids' initials on it. She's ironing her husband's clothes, with dinner cooking on the stove, all while bouncing a babbling baby on her hip. I die laughing watching it because I am nowhere near *any* of those things. I'm not sure there has ever been a day in our marriage that I have ironed my husband's clothes, nor even *thought* to. And cooking? Yeah, I mostly outsourced those responsibilities to him a long time ago. Or I'm really good at ordering. Occasionally, I'll follow a recipe when I'm feeling weird, but trust me, eliminating me from most food preparation responsibilities is better for everyone consuming the food.

I began to tackle other parts of me that weren't adding up to the model of a mom. There was NO part of me that wanted to be the classroom mom, the art docent, or even the field trip chaperone. I was not a Pinterest mom.

It was becoming abundantly clear at this point, as I continued to weed through what I was and wasn't, who I was and who I wasn't, that the mold just plain didn't fit. And instead of striving toward altering who I was, and making this whole square-peg round hole game try and work for the millionth time, I finally just said enough.

Enough!

I was never meant to fit the mold.

That was never going to bring me fulfillment. And it was never going to be who I was. I'm honestly not sure there is a mold that was meant to be fit into. I think the molds are BS. Aren't we past this in our generation yet? It was okay to stop trying. I was a bad ass, who happened to stay home with her kids as a career choice for now, but I also preferred to outsource kitchen and housework duties to someone better suited for the gig. Thankfully, that arrangement worked for my partner and I, and I needed to stop apologizing for it and feeling guilty, and step into it with confidence. There were other things I could do – who says a mom has to know how to cook?!

Oh, the freedom this started to bring me! I was learning to let go of the stereotypes, and the 'shoulds' of others, and was trading them in for unapologetic freedom and confidence. I started showing back up to my everyday life with a newfound sense of self. I didn't make noodle necklaces or spend hours playing busy toddler games in sensory bins of beans. I hated that crap and was tired of apologizing for it, and tired of *trying* to love it even though I clearly didn't.

My kids started picking up on this "new" mom, and they began to see me showing up each day in full color. On one particular colorful day, my oldest's teacher sent home a request for each student to bring in a batch of HOMEMADE frosting for their delightful gingerbread houses they were to be making the next day. Oh sweet Jesus, not the homemade again. My precious first-born son, God bless him, knew me well enough to pre-emptively raise his hand and ask if it was okay if his mom just bought the frosting. Yes Lord, I have done something right if he is asking this question – thank you for helping me, and him, to see the light of who I was made to be! Store bought all the way. His teacher's precious response, bless her, was NO. It must be homemade. ARE YOU JOKING ME?! Ugh. Sure, I would love to trade out my Monday night regular Bachelor watching agenda to make your precious homemade gingerbread house frosting. Nothing would please me more. *insert eye roll here* It honestly wouldn't have been *that* big of a deal if said recipe wouldn't have been calling for ingredients that most likely only could be found in the kitchen of the Pioneer Woman or Ina Garten. I don't just *have* flour and sugar and cream of tartar on hand – do you think I'm Joanna Gaines or something?! I'm sure every other normal elementary-kid mother just had to open a nicely labeled and organized cupboard to pull out their ingredients, but I was frantically googling what even the heck IS cream of tartar and can I substitute brown sugar or or applesauce or something for that? This one tiny task was sending me into an anxiety-ridden spiral. I quickly sent out an SOS to my neighborhood moms and begged for mercy to be shown upon me. Could someone PLEASE make my batch of required gingerbread house frosting for me? This was a desperate time. (*side note: teachers, I LOVE YOU. But please do not make such a LUDICROUS request during the holiday season when all of the women of the world are already expected to be the Executive Producer of all the magicalness of a child's Christmas. It is too much. Allow the store bought. Even if it means the freaking gingerbread house crumbles on the bus home. Crumbled gingerbread houses will be good life lessons for my kid to learn because no matter how magical that frosting is, you know that Gingerbread House is ending up in the trash can either way*).

Stupid right? But these are the things that are expected of women who stay at home. That they are good at, or at least have the ability, to just WHIP UP a nice batch of homemade special gingerbread house frosting with frankincense and myrrh and gold from the days of Jesus himself. No ma'am. Not this mom.

And as much as I laughed about it, those familiar thoughts of doubt and insecurity began to bubble up. This is my *job*, why can I not even pull myself together enough to make the damn frosting?

You guys, it just isn't my lane.

I was raised on boxed Velveeta shells and cheese and Hamburger Helper, so I partly have my parents to blame for my inadequacies in the domestic world. But I also have finally begun to just *embrace* that aside from my childhood and family of origin, God has *gifted* me in ways that just look a hell of a lot different than the world's version of a stay at home mom. I will never measure up or compare to those moms on Pinterest. And for those that are reading this that have followed my blog for years, you're probably thinking but you *look* exactly like the epitome of a Pinterest mom. Guys, it's a farse. That crap sucks the life out of me. Putting together a handmade birthday party full of scavenger hunts and themes with treasures waiting at the end of a rainbow? No thank you. I'd rather poke my eyes out. That sounds awful. Show up to a bouncy house place with Costco pizza and cheap Lego-themed plates and napkins from the Party Store? Now we're talking!

It's important to note that my official stance is definitely *pro* Pinterest moms (*please have this noted for the record*). My best friend is a Pinterest mom, and I *need* people like her. WE need people like her. She thrives with those themed little kid parties. And her kids will most likely need less counseling than mine due to their super magical childhood (*for real though, she makes it magical*). But if I try to keep up with her *natural giftings* in an area where I'm whatever the opposite of gifted is, then I'm going to keep hitting my head against a brick wall.

The description that I had been handed of what a stay at home mom was docile, precious, submissive. Yet the words that I related to best were Boss, CEO, COO, President. There was nothing docile about me.

Stay in your lane ladies. There's just no other way to navigate motherhood. I've tried. You will have SO MUCH life sucked out of you the more that you try and adjust your life, or way of living, to someone else's giftings. Identify your shortcomings, own them, and move on. This took me way too many years, and tears, to learn. The best thing that I ever did for myself was to discover my gifts and just lean in to those. I would encourage you to do the same. Once these are known and discovered by you, just stay there. Grow, yes. But none of this square-peg-round-hole BS. That's not who you were made to be, and that is OKAY. There is NO ONE who can do it all.

Trust that God has given you strengths and gifts that are good for *other* things which does not disqualify you from being a kick-A mom. If Pinterest parties and dolphin-shaped crustless sandwiches on the daily aren't your thing, that's OKAY. In fact, let me just call it out as GOOD. Cross that crap off the list, and quit doing it. Process of elimination is a great place to start with figuring out what will help you come alive in your day to day. Knowing what we're *not* good at is as important as knowing what we *are* good at. Lean into your strengths. Show your kids that yes, although sometimes we simply need to do what is needed (*aka make the damn homemade frosting*), it's okay to ask for help where you know you come up short. Call it out. Recognize it, and move on. You aren't good at hosting? Then, DON'T HOST. When you choose to do things out of obligation or expectation, I can promise you that it will breathe approximately ZERO life into you. And most likely even SUCK life out of you. Life is hard enough as it is, we were not meant to live everyday as if we're swimming upstream against the current. This is no way to live.

When I finally was able to come to terms with my lack of skills in the domestic world, it was then that Jesus was able to do His best work. Mostly on my heart. In the form of freedom. I was finally free to be me. All of me. Even the parts that weren't culturally approved, or celebrated. And it felt so damn good. I felt like me again.

This is how we are meant to live.

Free.

You possess skills and gifts that are very much on purpose. And they are purposeful for the specific kids that you are raising. The choice to set my career aside and stay at home to be with the kids in the little years full time was less a financial choice, and more a heart choice. Something inside my heart said home was where

I needed to be for this season. I didn't necessarily make the choice with a deadline in mind, eventually it did feel like a jail sentence more than a "calling", but I've been able to adjust my mindset and come out the other side to find the strength in spending this season with them. My kids need to see that strong, confident, non-domestic mom that God made me to be showing up every day in the exact way that He created me to be. What if my sole purpose is to show my daughter that you can be strong *and* raise a family, without having to collect a paycheck to fulfill your worth? What if my boys need to see a husband who cooks and cleans AND collects a paycheck? What if the way that we have chosen to divide our family roles, in a non-gender-stereotypical way, is the exact path that will lead *them* to freedom as they launch into the world? It became clear in our season of life currently that in our marriage, we each had a role: Blake makes the money, and I make the difference. Both were equal and needed. One isn't less than the other. It also isn't permanent. You do not have to try to fit a square peg in a round hole, and measure yourself up to someone else's standard; even if that person is in the same job as you are. This will only bring about feelings of doubt and questioning self-worth. Instead, do the things that make you light up. That bring *you* life. The things that you are naturally good at. THOSE are the things that you are meant to do. And as much as you can, let the guilt go when you outsource, or eliminate, the rest.

I have always said that I anticipate my wheelhouse being the teenage years. Late night talks, TP'ing, prom planning – it all sounds so dreamy *(clearly, I'm drunk)*. Stinky boys who just grunt a lot instead of using the words that I know they have learned. For some reason this has always been the season that I have known that I will thrive. This is partly why I do work with middle and high school kids through Young Life. I LOVE hearing about all the latest trends that the kids are doing these days and I want to just encourage them in all the things. Someone poured into me in that awkward phase of my life and I believe whole-heartedly that it set me on a path of confidence and self-belief that has served me so well. What a gift high schoolers are *(all high school moms are rolling their eyes HARD I know this)*. That phase of life gives many of my friends the exact same anxiety that I feel about homemade gingerbread house frosting. But even just talking about it gets me fired up and excited. Currently as I type, my children are three, five and seven so Lord help me because I still have a bajillion years until that blessed stage enters, but one thing I know for certain is that it will finally be my time to shine where feeding the children looks like Chik-fil-A drive-thrus and shoving sandwiches down your throat in between sports practices. Those are the domestic roles I was made for. But until then, I'm not going to let stereotypes and traditional gender roles tell me who I am or who I was made to be. I am a child of God and I am made perfectly just as I am. And so are you friend, so are you. Make the list. It's time to start celebrating and believing in who you *were* made to be, not who you weren't, because that's when it starts getting good.

CHAPTER 8

Wheel of Worthiness

I've always been a game show junkie my entire life. I'd have legit dreams and goals to be on every game show ever made. I'm one of those that sits at home and yells at the TV because clearly each contestant is A MORON compared to how I would perform if just given the opportunity. So years ago, I began applying to said gameshows. I'd answer random casting calls on Craigslist *(hello Newlywed game!),* and submit my online application for everything that I could possibly think of in hopes that my name and number would get called, I'd dominate the game, and then I could retire at the ripe old age of 23 with my $100,000 gameshow winnings.

Bless me.

Well newsflash, I haven't retired yet, but I did get the call on the bat phone years ago from Pat and Vanna. Yep, this was it. My big break...to audition. Even though the casting folks advised strongly against traveling to Los Angeles just for an audition, I told my boss in Seattle that I was headed for the bright shiny lights of Hollywood, and hopped a plane literally 48 hours later on my way to stardom.

When I arrived at my, what I assumed to be super elite casting call, I was in a bare hotel auditorium with about 75 other contestant hopefuls. I had received advice from a friend in the industry that puzzle solving ability was only a mere fraction of what they would be looking for. That ultimately they wanted someone to help make good TV, so I needed to act accordingly. As a former sorority girl, I knew just how to turn it up.

Our super exclusive *(read: they just pulled random people from the database who had LA addresses)* private audition consisted of a verbal test, a written puzzle test (no dummies allowed – this really surprised me) and a simulated game. As any good former sorority girl would, I gave them every bit of extra and polish that I had in me. And within 45 minutes, I got word - they had picked me! The only caveat was that I needed to be back in town to film within 24 hours. I will forever be thankful to my boss back home in Seattle for not even batting an eye when I called from LA and told him I would be flying home to work tomorrow, but that I was turning right back around to take my turn spinning the wheel on

Wheel of Fortune. I would need to miss work again the following day. I was so excited, I could hardly even stand it.

With my Grandma, my mom, my aunt, and my husband in tow, within 24 hours I was back on a plane to meet Pat and Vanna.

Upon arrival, I was grossly UNDERWHELMED with the level of hair and makeup they applied to me. I expected a full Pat & Vanna glam squad waiting to take me to the next level like I see when I'm Keeping Up With the Kardashians, but I had to do all my own hair and makeup. They simply applied a bit of extra powder to my less than amateur glam squad job because, well, two words: High Definition.

I was in a giant contestant pool, as they were filming six episodes that day, and each episode had three contestants, and a few backups in case someone got disqualified *(which WHAT? This basically instilled the fear of God in me)*. When it was finally my turn, my episode, we first did a warm up. They walked us out, met Pat & Vanna (inside scoop: they are not winning a dunk contest anytime soon if you catch my drift), and we had our turn to practice spinning the wheel. Wow! I quickly realized that I should've eaten my Wheaties that day because Lord have mercy, that wheel was HEAVY. The weight of the wheel, literally, caused me immediate panic. I totally panicked and lost my focus. All of a sudden everyone was staring at me, and I did what every at-home veteran yells about: *I bought a consonant.*

Oh my word the embarrassment. Everyone who has watched Wheel of Fortune ALWAYS laughs at those idiots who spin the wheel and then use their turn to say a vowel, when they are supposed to buy one. My husband later told me that he was dying of embarrassment in the audience while I humiliated myself during the practice round, and was ready to beeline it to the exit and not acknowledge that he was with me if I blew it during the real thing. Thanks babe. Putting those vows into practice, 'through good times and bad right?'

Anyway, right before we went on the air, I locked it in. The wheel wasn't super kind to me, but I was able to squeak out a few puzzles and within 20 minutes I was walking away with $7,200 in my pocket. Not quite the retirement fund I had envisioned, but not too shabby for twenty minutes worth of work. No, I didn't win (that was good enough to land me second place) but I was on cloud nine and felt like I just had won the lotto. I didn't rise to stardom (shocker), but when I went back home, I was able to tell friends and family who had known of my experience, all of the fun details. That was local celebrity status enough for me.

People were so surprised at this! How did you get on Wheel of Fortune? How did they choose you? Why? And basically after answering the question several times, I had a light bulb moment: why not me?

After living in LA for several years, I realized that everyone who had risen to stardom or was on TV or on a gameshow was just a normal person. A normal person who believed in a crazy adventure, enough to put themselves out there and just apply. Just try. And keep trying.

Motherhood is like trying to be on a game show. The primary difference is that the glam squad for motherhood looks vastly different than it did for even my small 15 minutes of fame for Wheel. Every day, we show up to try. Oftentimes, showing up is the very best that we can do – especially in those early days. You wonder if your effort to show up ever takes, or is seen by anyone, much like the countless applications I filled out for game shows. *Does anyone actually care that I'm doing this? Will anyone recognize my efforts? Will this even amount to anything?* For the most part, I think the monotony of motherhood will tell you no, your efforts don't amount to anything. Or at least that's what it will feel like. But then one day, your kid pushes in the chair without being asked, or goes to calm his little sister in an authentic way that shows you the true colors of their heart. And you think, Oh my! They actually DO listen! They are recognizing that I'm showing up for them day in and day out. Our efforts can feel like they are lost in the black hole of game show applications, with not a soul to survey our eligibility or superstardom, until one day, they call. And you wouldn't have ever gotten that call if you wouldn't have showed up every day. We don't know how this road of raising kids will go, and frankly, you could show up for months and years and they might walk away from this whole thing still giving you double middles. But that's on them. Your job is simply to keep showing up. You have to keep applying. Keep throwing your name in the hat. Keep throwing out kindness, and honesty, and patience, and love in the most reckless of ways. Because without reckless and wasteful love on the daily, we'll never even have the opportunity to realize the fruits of our labor. And like I said, showing up doesn't guarantee that we'll get to see that fruit – that's not promised to us at all – but we'll never know if we don't try.

Since Wheel of Fortune, I have continued to apply for several game shows. No one has called me since, but I apply for Ellen tickets every other week for going on seven years *(Side note: Ellen, if you're reading this, feel free to slide those tickets into my DM's)*. And someday, when she does call, it will appear as though it is seemingly random. Except it won't be. It will be the result of me applying faithfully week after week, not knowing the timing of when that phone will ring but trusting that if I keep at it, someday it will. Don't shelf your dreams, or desires, or ability to show up every day because your efforts appear or feel fruitless. Pursue them. Persevere after them. We have to believe in our wholeness and value because it is only then that we can trust that our efforts will not be in vain.

CHAPTER 9

Stay In Your Lane

Do you see what this means – all these pioneers who blazed the way, all these veterans cheering us on? It means we'd better get on with it. Strip down, start running – and never quit!

-Hebrews 12:1-2 (MSG translation)

One of the dumbest parts about being a mom in today's western American society is the notion that you can achieve it all. This is a big fat lie, and one I have fallen prey to too many times to count. Motherhood, marriage, parenting, job – it's all one big juggling act. And if you aren't careful, you will fall prey to the anxiety of feeling like you will are a failure on the daily, or your world will stop if God forbid, you drop a ball. It is a world of literally, impossible standards.

I am a humorous stay at home mom friend for my friends to have. I buck ALL of the stereotypes I'm sure, and I'm done apologizing for it. Don't even try and label me because it won't work. I once heard the phrase "Somewhere between Proverbs 31 and Tupac, there's me." And I thought yasssss, NOW someone finally gets me. But it's the truth.

Being a mom *is* enough.

And yet, it is rare in my social circles right now to come across a woman who just does one thing. There is a pressure to not just raise your kids well, but also to maintain a weekly date night in order to be at thriving marital status *(when let's be honest, most of us are just surviving)*, volunteer in the classroom, initiate happy hour with your girlfriends on the regular, contribute in a significant way to your local philanthropy of choice, keep up those hair roots when the greys pop through every 4-6 weeks, oh AND have a healthy well-balanced nutrient rich meal prepped morning, noon, and night for each of the tiny humans residing in your household. And the list of pressures goes on. I'm sure you could rattle off at least 17 more if we sat down for coffee.

I'm sort of tired of it though. I'm tired of the pressures that say we need to do it all, be it all, and have it all. I'm tired of feeling like whatever it is that I have chosen as a vocation or life choice (which is full time motherhood at this point) needs to also be accompanied by something else in order to gain approval or acceptance.

Ladies, let's just focus on ONE thing and trust that it is enough. If you believe it for yourself, and present your one thing with pride, there is no room for judgement or feelings of not enough. There is no rule at how often you can change up this thing. All of you in one thing is *so* much better than part of you in lots of things.

Being a mom is enough.

Being a wife is enough.

Being a teacher is enough.

Running a big or small business is enough.

You do not have to do it all, nor do I recommend it. Mind you, I recognize fully that we are all *capable* of doing more than one thing. I am an Achiever on the Enneagram after all, getting things done is my go-to. But just because we *can* doesn't mean we *should.* Multi-tasking is a myth and frankly in my opinion has gotten way out of hand in our distracted state of living these days. When is the last time that you just let yourself do one thing at a time? Watch TV without a device or computer on your lap? Not turned the channel during the commercial just to fill the "empty" space. Just sat at a red light instead of grabbing your phone to mindlessly scroll or check your likes for two minutes?

For me, the story I tell myself is not extremely positive very often. I become consumed with "not doing enough" and just overall "not enough-ness". That I could be doing more and that my efforts aren't worthwhile. This is what is referred to as the "shadow" side of an Enneagram three. They tell me my core fear is to be/feel worthless. I'll be honest, this voice is louder than I care to admit today – the one that questions my worth. I feel frustrated and alone. But I refuse to let the world define my worth and tell me it's not good enough. That I need to be doing *more* as a mom. So instead, I'm choosing to believe that I was made for more. And I am enough not because of what I DO, but more in WHOSE I am. In the book of Genesis in the Bible, scripture tells me that I was made in the image of God and that I don't have to do anything to earn his love. We came out of the womb with infinite value and worth already assigned to us. It is something that is a truth in which we don't have to question how or why or if – it just is. A constant. And if I choose to believe that I am whole and worthy at my deepest core, in my deepest self, then everything that I *do* beyond that comes from a place of abundance instead of place of seeking validation or value from my efforts. When I choose to believe and accept that I am loved wholly for who I am, the ugly parts and all, then I am freed up to pour out love to the little terds in my care without needing them to say, "Good job". When I choose to let that level of wasteful love *in,* it frees me up to begin to let that type of reckless love *out.*

Hear me when I say that nothing that you DO will ever be enough to earn approval or worth from anyone. We have got to stop striving. There is no magical balance, there is no magical arrival point. Let's band together and encourage one another in the one, two, or 30 things that we each do well. And then we must go beyond the achievements and call out things in our lives that are character-based. We all want someone to affirm in us that we are okay. That we are doing okay. Friends, you are doing better than you think.

Really receive that.

Those little people ADORE you. Trust me, I know that they yell at you all day long. If they're anything like mine, your daily routines feel more like a gong show rather than an environment of adoration, success, or appreciation. But the women ahead of all of us say it's true; they don't see the 10,000 things on your to-do list that you didn't get done this week, this month or this year. The kids see YOU. We don't need to *do* in order to *be*. And in fact, I've learned that my being, in whatever state that is, has to be the first step of acceptance before I can do anything else that is of genuine value and vulnerability. I first have to accept me before I can *do* anything else.

Can you imagine if one of your little's came up to you and expressed some of the things that we as women allow ourselves to think? That they weren't good enough. That they had no purpose for being here. Your heart would break and you would be crushed.

Now I am a person of faith; specifically, I look to the teachings and life of Jesus as written in the Bible as guidance. And I can't really write this book or write this story for you without letting you in on the source of truth for me, and source of affirmation for me in my battle back to finding and re-discovering my identity.

Jesus is the Father that looks at you, his daughter, in the exact same way that you would respond to one of your kids if they told you they weren't good enough. His heart breaks for you as your head swirls with self-doubt and negative self-talk because you've dropped yet another ball for the day. You yelled at your kids more than you hoped, and totally lost your cool, and now you are so down on yourself. That is not how God sees you. You are his worthy and purposeful creation with whom he looks at with only the adoration that a parent can have. As any loving Father would, it breaks his heart to see you, his worthy and purposeful creation, and it kills him to hear you speak these untruths, even in your subconscious narrative.

If you are like me, and find yourself in a job, career or life situation that you didn't plan or prepare for, and you are struggling to figure out what your *thing* is, what it is that you were made to do, or what it is that you have to contribute that only you can contribute, can I encourage you just for a minute? We have to stop searching for this elusive "thing" outside of what you are already doing, and rest in the truth that even without the accomplishments or achievements, that your simple being here and showing up to love your people is enough. Your paycheck, or lack thereof, does not determine your worth. How many likes or followers you have on social media will not bring satisfaction or contentment if you don't first accept who you were created to be. And right now, at least part of that, is a mom. You were created for this role. You were created for this job. And all of the other outside things – career, side hustles, likes, follows, tweets, awards – will not change the status of your heart unless you first accept for yourself that you are enough.

And maybe you're sitting there reading this and saying, "But Ashley, okay fine, I do believe that what I am doing right now as a mom is enough, but I want more – I have a dream in my heart that I want to pursue but I'm not sure how to find it or what it exactly looks like." And for you sister, I say, "Let's figure it out." Once you have accepted the basic truth, then yes, let's start working toward discovering the thing that you were made to create and share with the world. If you are unsure what it is, I'd start by asking some of your people. Ask them, 'What is it that you think I'm good at?' 'What do you see me doing well in my life?' 'What are areas that you hear me gripe about?' 'When are times when you see me come alive?' I recognize this is a really vulnerable question, but I pray that you have the bravery and courage to ask just one or two or three of your trusted people. And be ready to receive whatever it is they have to say. Listen for the patterns. Receive their positive assessments of you with gratitude and humility. Because I believe in Jesus, I also believe that there is an ultimate enemy of our soul. And sometimes, I believe that the enemy wants us to be walking around with blinders on to what it is that we are naturally gifted at so that we are perpetually stuck in a constant state of discontent and apathy. This way, we don't play our part and don't contribute what we're meant to contribute. Or at the very least, we are distracted and that keeps us from contributing what our thing is as well!

To this day, I still find myself getting caught up in the stuff, in the things, in the pursuit of the things as my means to validate my worth and value. I am quicker to catch myself in these lies and go back to the truths about who I am, and *Whose* I believe I am, but it's not something that I have arrived on. I still struggle with it. I mean goodness, it's taken me nearly three years to write this book! Why? Because every time I'd be in a good place mentally, I would feel that confidence in me surging and I'd begin to put words on the page to share with you (*and for me*), but the minute that I put my hope in my circumstances that this thing would bring me purpose or value, I'd shut it down. I'd go back and continue to do the work of integration and self-discovery and acceptance for everything that I was created to be, without any of the 'do'. I'd return to the basic idea that my people right in front of me, including myself, had to be the mission for my greatest work. Because we can't pursue the things outside of motherhood while neglecting the people right in front of us. And if we buy into the lie that pouring ourselves into our work, or our vocation, is more noble or worthy of a cause than our people, then I think we've bought into a false truth.

I don't believe that I will get to heaven's gate one day and wish that I would have scrolled on my phone one minute longer. I'm not going to wish that I had stayed in my fancy career or pursued that side hustle with one more hour, if it meant neglecting who I was or the people in my home. Remember, this is a season. Do I think that you can have a fancy career AND be a good mom? OF COURSE! They are not mutually exclusive and I most definitely do not subscribe to the idea that one path is better than the other. I just know that for me, I had to be stripped down of my achievements and accolades, and accept the girl in the mirror for who I was – muffin top and all – before I could stretch my wings outside of motherhood. I needed motherhood to help me come to the very end of myself and surrender, so that I could truly find me – and be happy with her! So that I could root my identity in something greater than me, not just a circumstance or vocation or idea of one.

It is okay to focus on just one thing, which might just be motherhood for you right now. The world will tell you this is not okay and that you need to be achieving a lot more. I call BS. Motherhood can be your one thing, it is enough. Maybe now is not the timing for you to do the side hustles and motherhood and the fancy career. Maybe for you, being a mom is the only thing that you need to pour into right now because that's where you're at. For me, this has been true for so long. And I have fought it for so long because I thought that as an educated woman of the 21st century that it was my responsibility, or that I was a failure if I wasn't doing more. Surely, I *needed* to be doing more than momming 24/7. But what I actually needed to understand and believe is that I already *was* more than a mom. Motherhood didn't define me. God does.

CHAPTER 10

It Doesn't Add Up

Dreaming is not just for dreamers. We are all built to be dreamers. In Jennie Allen's book *Restless,* she asks the question, "When you anticipate dreaming, what are you afraid of?" For me, the answer was failing. Not having something significant to offer anyone anymore. This ultimately, when dissected, was rooted in my misconception of my worth. And valuing *ability* more than *being*.

As a white female raised in a well-to-do suburban country club town (*eye rolls are warranted, I get it*), much of the emphasis of my community and surrounding culture was on achievement, as you can imagine. It was assumed that everyone would be striving toward college. And then ultimately the mark of great success at each level was achieving those goals at the highest level. Awards, accolades, prestige – all of it was expected and highly celebrated. It wasn't good enough to just play sports, you had to play year-round sports on a "select" team. It wasn't enough to simply pursue higher education, you needed to get in to the *best* school. Once in school, there was pressure for internships each summer and to achieve social status within your friend groups. For me, I was good at all these things, so it came naturally for me. I was a natural leader, a good kid, school came fairly easy for me, and thus the achievements and success followed.

This carried into adulthood as I was amongst the very first to land a GREAT guy, get married and find a dream job right away in Los Angeles. I want to stop you right there, because I know what you're thinking – this sounds like SUCH a tragic story Ashley, what is your POINT? My point is that I had no clue that even though I claimed to be a follower of Jesus, that my identity and worth was completely and entirely wrapped up in my achievements. Success, being liked, captain of my sports teams always, in the popular crowd, these were all things that I began in subtle ways, to wrap my identity in, along with the continued success of them. I became addicted to the admiration and affirmation that achieving brought to me – without even consciously knowing it. The desire to climb, grow and be at the top is something that is so celebrated in our culture. Hard work to get what you want is the American dream, and we are taught this from a very young age. The problem arises though when we aren't affirming or working on our character. When our achievements are what bring us praise and glory, slowly but surely the eggs start to pile up in that basket because it gives us a quick hit of feeling good – a little dopamine every time you "hit the mark". Except, the quick hit is just that – it's not actually a lasting feeling of value, security or worth.

It has taken me a lot of years to realize that I was addicted to this achievement mentality. And frankly, it has taken me a lot of *work* to finally connect the dots as to why my entire emotional psyche has come completely unraveled since choosing to stay at home and raise the kids. All of my achievement was gone. All of my accolades, toast. I was suddenly thrown *(I use that term lightly because well, I did get pregnant and ask for that role)*, into a world with no affirmation and working for people who didn't care what my degree was, how successful I had been in my previous day job, or that I had the ability to do WAY bigger and cooler things than cooking them chicken nuggets for the third meal in a row. Stripped away unbeknownst to me. I was fully immersed in what felt like was an ongoing Groundhog's Day, where there was no praise, award or recognition for the diapers I was changing, the crumbs I was cleaning up and the laundry I was washing. Not only that, but it just felt like a job that was *beneath* me. That's embarrassing to admit, but it definitely is the truth. I thought for many years that I was *too good* to be doing such menial tasks. Why would you call me here God? I have SO much more to offer! I am smart, and competent, and can crush it in the office – isn't that more valuable? Wouldn't you rather have me "being a light" (*it's a Christian term that is silly really because we all are light-bearers, hence the quotes)* in the workplace, than at home here with these maniacs who DON'T EVEN FREAKING APPRECIATE ME?!

But oh, sister of mine who just said YEAH, this just isn't how the world works when we serve a good God. And trust me, I say that from a place of FRICK, that sucks for me too.

One of my favorite stories in the Bible is the story that I'm sure you have heard 1,000 times if you have been in or near church at all. But if not, cuddle up, I'll give you some cliff notes *(in the Ashley translation)*. It is the story of when Jesus feeds 5,000 people. The story has slightly different variations according to each author of the Gospels in the New Testament section of the Bible, but in John chapter 6, we read that after Jesus' closest friends *(bible vocab word for the day: disciples = Jesus' friends)* let Jesus know there is a giant crowd who are all going to be super hungry real soon, and they are stumped at how they are going to feed them. They suggest going out and *purchasing* enough food to feed them, but aren't positive that they'll have enough money for that. Some other wise guy has the brilliant hospitable idea to just send everyone home so that they can buy their own food *(this would've for sure been my suggestion – tell them to go feed themselves; I'm super compassionate)*. Jesus says no, hogwash *(Ashley interpretation)*. He wants his friends to be responsible to feed the hungry people. Ugh, I'm sure they were thinking, "WE have to do it?! But YOU'RE God – why don't you just feed them?!" When they accept the directive from Jesus, they look around to figure out where they're going to find enough food. I believe this is where the phrase "faith like a child" may have come from, but a brave little boy comes forward and offers what he has: five loaves of bread and two fish. I'm not sure the last time that you went to a dinner party, but if I showed up with 5,000 of my closest friends for a meal and saw that there was only 2 measly fish and 5 loaves of bread, I'd for sure think we had a problem. Someone was definitely going hungry, or more like 4,999 *someone's* and it was NOT going to be me.

But in this moment of presumed need and conundrum, Jesus takes what this little boy has to offer, prays over it and asks God to bless it, instructs his friends to ask everyone to sit down on the grass in groups, and then begins passing the baskets of bread and fish around. As the story goes, it says that everyone ate until they were satisfied and had had as much as they wanted (John 6:11).

They ate until they were full. And there were leftovers. I'm not a math major *(this is more my husband's department)*, but it seems to me that 5+2 *does not* equal 5,000. But somehow in God's upside down economy, it does. And in reality, it actually fed *more than* 5,000 because it's recorded in the book of Matthew that there were women and children there as well, but for whatever reason they weren't "counted" back then *(don't even get me started on that – that'll be my next book)*.

How can the seemingly very little that we have, when laid down and submitted to God, be enough? It makes no sense. I don't know the why or how behind it, I simply know it as truth. The only explanation I have is that it's miraculous. And I have seen it to be true true time and again in my own life. To me, it reads as a message of radical abundance about the character of God. When I read it, I feel hopeful. It gives me hope that little old me, stay at home mom of three in Seattle, who has audacious dreams of influencing a generation and standing on stages and getting weekly blowouts because I CAN, but is stuck here folding laundry and wiping butts and runny noses, *will* actually maybe get to see a day where my little story, message and influence, transforms and gets used to help many. And gets used to help many of whom I will never know and meet. It gives me hope that the dreams that are buried way down deep in my heart for a life full of legacy and generosity that don't make any sense and are seemingly so outlandish and out of reach right now from where I stand, can actually mean something someday. That the monotonous hours I spend every day parenting *(close your mouth when you chew; push in your chair; say I'm sorry; we don't use our hands to solve our problems)*, like real everyday grind-it-out parenting, might actually mean something meaningful in the world someday. Not because we were all built for stages, but because the "little" that we have can be multiplied in ways that are far beyond our control and comprehension. The butts that you are wiping today or the endless years of diaper changing that you are staring down right now as you come home from the hospital, they are going to add up. And not necessarily to big things the way the world defines big, but moreso to beautiful things in all of the ways that really matter. The work inside our four walls – both the physical labor and the emotional heavy lifting we do in parenting – it matters. There is no task beneath us. The sticky and messy floors that you're sweeping and mopping yet again are holy ground for humans that will someday bring light forward in the world. They're holy ground for you as you become, and transform, into women who lead with empathy and compassion, grit and tenacity.

So every day, when I am struggling, feeling like I have skills or gifts in me that aren't being utilized in this season of life, and then spiraling down the tunnel of feeling inadequate in my worth because "all" I'm doing is vacuuming up crumbs for the 400th time, maybe I need to take an Econ lesson from Professor Jesus. How would things begin to change for me if I were to submit the daily tasks, the small things that are required of everyday moms, the unseen things that motherhood demands of us, and ask God to bless it, use it, grow it, and make it count? Maybe I can't yet see the world changer whose butt I am wiping and reading that book to for the thousandth time today. Maybe I can't yet see the mom who I run into every day at preschool watching how I parent my kids and seeing glimpses of Jesus' love, craving it for herself or her kids too. Guys, I don't have a lot to offer. I'm just me. If being a mom has taught me anything, it's humility. All of those things that I accomplished in my previous life, they don't matter in the long run. Yet, God can take it and change an entire generation. An entire neighborhood. An entire community. An entire family. An entire life. No matter the scale, the work is worth it. The obedience to show up and simply put one foot in front of the other is worth it.

If you feel like the place where you are at right now is inadequate, I feel you sister. I have spent so many years feeling those feelings. And very much still feel them in my every day. What I learn from this story though, is that achievement, or having a lot or doing a lot is not necessarily going to be the catalyst to what gets you to your goals. This is a backwards, upside down economy. The last will be first. And a massive crowd of 5,000 people can be fed with leftovers with only seven pieces of food.

It *appears* like you have nothing to offer but sister, it's a lie.

You have *something*.

If you have breath in your lungs, there is *something* that you have to offer, regardless of the awards, job or special skills you think you might possess (or not possess). I'm just the messenger here, test it for yourself. Bring forth the little that you have. Work at it with purpose and pride. The little person. The little vision. The singular voice. And watch.

God does not call the equipped, he equips the called. Adequacy does not equal worth. And purpose does not equal worth. Your worth rests only in the God who has the ability to feed 5,000 from a boy's offering of virtually nothing. And I promise He will show up the same for you. I've seen it firsthand. I believe it. And days when you don't believe it, head back to his words and see how he has proven his faithfulness time and again. This will bring you freedom. You can trust that your little can, and will be, more than you can see right now in the weeds.

CHAPTER 11

Laugh More, Laugh Often

"I used to have functioning brain cells, but then I traded them in for having children"-Ecards

Someone please tell me what is better than a solid laugh sesh? I recently was on a YouTube video binge of some SERIOUSLY funny people and I got to the point where I had literal, actual tears streaming down my face. Melissa Radke, James Corden, Heatherland, and John Crist I'm looking at you. I told my husband later that evening that I'm convinced there is nothing better for your soul than laughter. It has the ability to change my mood in an instant.

When we went from having two kids to adding the third, and suddenly it was fulltime zone-defense, I was faced with a choice: I could lose my ever-loving mind at the 24/7 chaos that was my life, or I could embrace the chaos and just start laughing. Most days, I tried to choose laughter. Baby blowout ALL over my clothes in a restaurant while nursing? Laugh it off. Naked toddler in public because we're potty training and she needed to go RIGHT NOW? Laugh it off. Oh sure, I received all sorts of stares from judgmental clearly-never-had-children-eyes, but I was so deep in the parenting trenches that I was past caring and had zero effs to give what they thought of me.

I'm no scientist, but I'm pretty sure your brain lights up with rainbows and Skittles when you start laughing, which most likely makes some sort of neuron start firing off positive thoughts. Again, very scientific. Botox and magical anti-aging serums and creams will have nothing on the amount of laugh wrinkles and lines I aim to have all over my face when it's time for Jesus to call me to Heaven. I'm going to consider that a win, and the laugh wrinkles on my face will be my measuring stick. There isn't anything else out there that can pull me back from the depths of despair from a day at home with three maniacs, than laughter. Pissed off at life? Turn on Ellen and I dare you to not change the trajectory of your day immediately. Fed up with the never-ending grind of chores and people you're responsible for? Watch an episode of Carpool Karaoke and see how your mood shifts. It's contagious. And magical. Laughter is the unicorn of life. Humor is something that I value and need.

If you want to experience a purposeful journey through motherhood, laughter is a must. The exact way we choose to spend our days, is the exact way that we choose to spend our life. The monotony and boredom of the everyday life of managing three kids is enough to make me want to poke my eyes out. Not because there's a lack of things to do. Au contraire, it is in fact the opposite. All the things to do are just really boring! The individual tasks and responsibilities of running and managing a household is freaking boring to me. Also, there is SO much to do, and SO many needs that I just want to escape from them all. I want to ignore them all and run away. Yes, I know, many clinical therapists probably would call this depression. And on some level, it is. Just high functioning depression, if that's such a thing.

One thing I put on my calendar regularly to combat this is something FUN. If I don't have something fun to look forward to, I guarantee you will find me in the fetal position somewhere near a fireplace or on the bathroom floor, rocking back and forth. Survival of motherhood is not possible without a little bit of fun. I didn't realize how much of a value fun was for me until I became a mom and had little minions running around all day long that sucked the LIFE out of me. Fun doesn't just happen though. It is a myth that fun things *just happen* to fun people. Sure, you can always choose laughter in the middle of a diarrhea blowout, but true fun, won't just fall into your lap. Fun for me, is the act of releasing so much of the work and tension and stress that come along with my day (and night) job. Yes, the work that we are doing at home is so good (*read: hard!*) and purposeful, but without the act of releasing, you will head toward burnout city. And we can't have that.

Fun is the antidote for me for burnout. It just requires some serious intentionality though – you must schedule it in order to make it happen. Local concerts? Check! Renting a comedy on your Netflix or OnDemand? Check! Going on a girl's weekend? Check, check! You NEED these things in order to remember who you are outside of the home, or raising your kids. And for me, every time I do something that makes me laugh, or is just simply out of the daily monotony, it reminds me that I'm alive and that I enjoy life! (*Oh BT dubs, I'm no doctor but this is prob a good depression antidote*). I come across so many mom friends, both who work inside and outside of the home, who just don't feel like they *deserve* to carve out the time to have fun anymore. Are you kidding me?! On what Earth does someone who works literally 7 days a week not deserve to go out and do something fun, *on the regular?!* It's like for some reason, as women, we have guilted or shamed ourselves into believing that doing these things isn't worthwhile or worthy, or deserved. Well someone hand me a box of soap because those dishes, that laundry, that damn Leprechaun trap school project – it'll all still be there to be done every single day of your life. If you don't make the conscious choice to put it aside for just a moment in order do something fun right now, or at least within the next month, I promise you that rat wheel will keep spinning.

It will never stop until you *choose* to jump off. As long as we choose to stay on the rat wheel with productivity as our highest value, there will not be a left-hand turn that just comes your way for fun.

Recently, there have been an influx of movements created by women whom I will deem as the epitome of fun moms. Oh man, I LOVE these women for using their humor to bring life to the mom world. People like Cat & Nat, IMomSoHard and Melissa Radke are basically freaking geniuses and if you don't yet know their work, put this book down right now and go look them up on YouTube and Instagram. They will make you feel NOT CRAZY and completely normal. Those days when you feel like your life is one complete gong show, they are there to remind you that every other mom who is also in your same phase of life is walking a similar path of crazy. And if you don't think so, then your people are DAMN good at hiding it. Because I guarantee no one has it all together.

Humor and fun are a gift. They are the release where beauty & joy enter life and for a moment, your heart and chest will feel a bit lighter from the load that you are carrying. As women, we need to be having fun. The load of motherhood is just too weighty to carry on our own, without regular and consistent releases. Good lord can you imagine getting to the pearly gates *(I recognize this is the second time that I have referenced arrival at the pearly gates – I just legit think about this moment all the time)* and feeling *super* dumb about all those dishes and laundry you spent your days and nights doing, when you should've been out there living? Sometimes the logistics don't make sense. It will cost you something, it doesn't always come for free. But some of my most favorite memories of motherhood are the times when we threw caution to the wind and just lived. With, or without, the kids present. ▯

I can remember a specific time when laughter and giggles triumphed. It was a school night, and I was out with two of my best girlfriends. Collectively between the three of us, we have eight kids, so a mom's night out of dinner, drinks, and a movie was on the docket. For us at this point, casual girls night out was something fairly normal and regular because escapism is a regular coping mechanism for me while raising teeny tinies. Not like weekly date night regular, but we always were conscious, especially in the teeny tiny years raising our littles in the weeds, to get out. With dinner and drinks under our belt, we headed to the movies. Very cliché of us, we chose to see some easily forgotten chick flick, and it was cute and fun and we walked out of the theater feeling good about our decisions. But as soon as we walked out, a wave of rebellion washed over one of us. I can't remember precisely which one of us had the flash of brilliance, but suddenly against every good suburban mom code, we decided to sneak in to the late night showing of Bad Moms! I know what you're thinking – gosh Ash, you guys are crazy! And to that I say, "it gets really real out here in the 'burbs." I don't think I had ever giggled as hard as I did trying to pretend like we for sure had a ticket and belonged in that theater. I couldn't tell you the titles of the last five movies that I've seen in the theater *(okay, actually I did see The Greatest Showman, and it was uh-maze!)*, but I will always remember sneaking in to Bad Moms. It was with that same group of girls several months later that we were out for dinner one night, sans kids *(which if you know me, this is ALWAYS my first choice...sans kids)*, and we shut the restaurant down. Except we weren't done hanging out. And that familiar rush of Suburban Rebellion came sweeping over us yet again. Truly, don't even try to get in the way of a stay-at-home mom who hasn't had uninterrupted adult time in weeks. We were mamas on a mission...to keep having fun! So we surveyed our surroundings, and decided the local QFC was the next best place for us to continue our night's festivities. We made our way in like any normal grocery shopper, except we took a hard right up the stairs of the store and promptly made ourselves at home in the Employee Lounge. We let ourselves in past the Employees Only sign like we owned the joint. There were several employees who came up to use the restroom, or get something out of the fridge, and they were so confused by these three giggly moms camping out at midnight in their break room. But we didn't care. We were having the time of our life and again giggling until at least one of us possibly tinkled in our underpants a bit.

I don't think you need to be breaking laws in order to have fun. But you do need your people. And you do need to just get out there and do it. The feelings of suffocation can easily drown out the everyday with the monotony of a nap schedule, or early bedtimes, or quarantined sick kids. Don't let those things, those circumstances, rob you of the joy that you can experience in life. Stop making excuses for why you can't go out, why you can't hang out. Fun is part of your mental health and survival regiment. Sometimes you need to be goofy and sit in a break room, or sometimes you just need to turn on Jimmy Fallon. I don't want to wake up in twenty years when my kids are grown and gone, without having had my own joys and laughs to look back on. You are your own person. Laughter is great self-care, and for sure a worthwhile investment and way to spend your time. Your girlfriends are part of that. Find them, be them, and gather them. And if you're reading this and thinking, "But I don't have any friends" well sister, we'll cover that. Because you need them. We were made to be connected in relationship with others and I'm not going to let the excuse of no friends keep you from having fun and living a full life. Cindy didn't sing it for her health, she really meant it when she said "Girls just wanna have fun." *(Oh girls, just wanna have fun. That's all they really waaaaannnnttttt).*

CHAPTER 12

Parenting in the Trenches

I'm an introvert by nature, or maybe I'm extroverted introvert *(I'm still working this out)* so most of the time I LOVED and needed the blessed time that came every day called nap time. But once or twice a week, I would gladly welcome a friendly interruption. My friends who were also at home (even just on weekends) quickly became my lifeline. I think it's a lie that you assume your mom-friend probably is too busy to hang out. I can all but guarantee that she is lonely AF. If not on her schedule, at least in her soul. Since I know this personally and intimately, I just always assume it for others oftentimes as well and began being the initiator; like a friend-bridge of sorts.

When we are alone in isolation is precisely the moment when we are so vulnerable to allowing lies to creep in. Those familiar lies surrounding doubt, self-worth, purpose, identity. Believing the lie that the highlight reel of social media that you spend time scrolling through at naptime really IS what their life looks like. And yours sucks in comparison. Social media is not real life and it is not real connection. Okay, I take that back – I definitely have made real connections via social media. But it is not a full substitute for real actual humans that you let in to your everyday life. We can't let ourselves be known, and build entire connections in 15 second increments and tiny collages of perfectly-filtered squares. Social media itself is not garbage and does not need to be lit on fire. But the lies of stories that we begin to tell ourselves when we scroll - those are what need to get thrown into the garbage. This is when the enemy of our soul subtly creeps in. Do not fight this enemy in isolation. We must be in community with one another instead of living on our own islands of loneliness. Throwing a life raft to a friend looks as simple as linking arms and tackling the trenches together. Raising kids is freaking hard. I promise you that there is a friend in your life that might not *look* like she needs your companionship, but I can promise you would relish genuine connection and friendship in her everyday.

In the early days of parenthood, some of my most favorite days during the week were the impromptu playdates, that then turned in to husbands joining us for impromptu dinner, and next thing we knew, we'd spent the better half of an entire today parenting, without it ever feeling like parenting. Our pack-n-play lived in the back of our car, and we were not afraid to put the rug rat down for a nap, or for the night while we were at a friend's house (*so as to keep his schedule in place of course!*), so that we didn't have to sacrifice time with our people. These friendships, these relationships, are crucial for the success of our parenting careers. Not only that, but for whatever reason, parenting in the trenches with other people just feels like a much lighter load. You realize that your personal gong show, is actually a collective gong show, and instead of yelling or retreating in frustration from the threenager tantrum yet again, you simply laugh for what it really is – absurd. There's a *reason* why moms who have weathered these little years don't talk about them in great detail. Because they're freaking hard! I'm pretty sure the trauma of poop in the bathtub on the regular, constant time outs, and perpetual whining just gets locked in the blackout section of our brains, right there next to childbirth. You want joy in your day to day? You want to laugh and feel like your current load is lighter? Call up a friend. Invite them in, mess and all. Plan for an extended stay (big fan of adult slumber parties too!), and just do normal life together. Order pizza. Get takeout. Open a bottle of wine and turn on a movie for the kids. Life is better together. Each of us has so much to offer one another and we can't do it alone.

This also requires us to admit that we need help. Moms of little's, when a mom who has already walked your path ahead of you, offers help in the form of a meal, a playdate with one of your kids, to rock your baby to sleep, an impromptu night out for drinks, RECEIVE IT. This is a gift and a life raft. They see you and your struggle. They know that hole you're in, they see you down there in the ditch, living out a constant Groundhog Day. And they want to help. And they'll offer to help in the manner in which they wish someone would've shown up for them when they needed it. And if you're lucky enough to be past the season of naptimes and daily trenches, then you get the privilege to be the friend that you wish you had during those long days. Showing up for one another is how we do this mom thing better. Just show up. Don't ask HOW you can help, oftentimes it looks like just showing up. That's what doing life together means. Anticipating the needs of others and serving them. It will be a gift to you as the giver, *and* it will be a gift to the receiver.

A few years ago, when deciding where we really wanted to raise our kids and put down roots for the long haul, we circled through what is now our current neighborhood one sunny afternoon, and fell in love. The only problem was that there were no houses for sale. We immediately went balls to the wall savage on networking, sending out postcards, and walking the 'hood like a bunch of creepers hoping to just "come across" someone washing their car or mowing their lawn outside, who was also looking to sell their house. The odds of this being successful felt small. And we looked like total weirdos. We had very specific requirements or hopes *(none of which were rooted in anything other than desire)* and spent a solid year and a half praying over these things and hitting the ground hard. We believed that if this is where we were supposed to be, the door would be open.

Sure enough, after our second round of mailers to these not-on-the-market houses, one day the sweetest elderly couple who had raised their six kids in this neighborhood, emailed us with an olive branch – they were looking to sell! I remember when Blake read the email, he immediately called me just freaking out with excitement and anticipation because on paper *(because yes, you can find most all pertinent facts about a house including how much they owe and if they've ever done a major remodel online – you can add 10 more points to the Carbonatto creeper column)* this house seemed to fit the bill and check off every box that we had hoped for. We had sent the mailers targeting location primarily, but this was the part we didn't know how to navigate – what did our interactions look like? I remember I wanted to put our very best foot forward when we went to go tour the house. This was an off market deal, no real estate agents were involved and we were walking into what felt like the most massive interview to potential buy these people's house. I put my boys in their best collared shirts, put pigtails in the little one's hair, grabbed a grocery store bouquet of flowers and we went to tour the house. Pulling up, I had so many nerves. *What would they think of us? We didn't even know what this house looked like on the inside! How much would they ask? Would it be way outside of our budget?* But with one step inside, we knew: this was our dream house. There was brown shag carpet everywhere, original parquet wood floors, linoleum and vinyl flooring in several spaces and it just screamed I NEED A FACELIFT! We spent hours with this elderly couple, letting them relive their entire 38 years that they had lived there, sharing with us all their highlights from raising their kids in the home. We shook hands as we left, and as we climbed into our car both Blake and I looked at each other and said, "I think we just bought a house!"

Several months later, we got the keys to our 1970's dream home and began demo that very first day. We were able to fully gut our house and do a full remodel (*in hindsight, we should've just torn the whole thing down but whatevs*) and still be way under market and within our desired budget. We felt so fortunate, and continually pinched ourselves.

This neighborhood is what suburban dreams are made of. Kids everywhere. Tennis courts. Parks. Bike trails. A private beach on the lake. It's as dreamy as it sounds, I promise. But I tell you this not to make you jealous, but simply because we had NO BUSINESS getting the house that we did, for the price that we did, in the neighborhood that we did. Other than the fact that our hands and lives were open to receive. Our heart's desire was to build community by demonstrating radical hospitality right where we were at. By just doing normal life. The easiest way that I know how to find purpose is through our regular everyday lives.

There was a catch though: shiny circumstances don't bring us lasting contentment or purpose. We had finally moved in, we had the house, we were in the neighborhood, but I had no friends. Enter that familiar friend to everyday moms: loneliness. Even though we had only moved about 45 minutes from our previous house, it was a far enough distance that all my previous mom-stomping grounds were no longer applicable. Different library, different parks, different walking routes – I had lost my everyday close-in-proximity friends who were my go-to for impromptu daily life. In the trenches of motherhood, proximity is key for many of your friendships.

Making friends in your thirties though just doesn't look the same as it does in your college years, or even in your twenties – especially if you don't have a workplace outside of the home to go to. And on top of that, my oldest was entering into the world of Kindergarten at the local public school and that was super intimidating from a social perspective. Not only was he going to be the new kid, *I* was going to be the new kid! Being the new mom, in an already-established crew, is so hard! Talk about recipe for anxiety. I had no choice though; it was time to put on my big girl panties and make friends. You move to a new 'hood, and people seem to have their crew. I knew one person in my new neighborhood from before and she made me promises of invites into Book

Clubs, Bunco, and the neighborhood Dad group. I was so excited. Except when we moved in, these promised invites were nowhere to be found. It was crickets from her. At first, I was bitter and legit hurt – mostly because I was so desperate to begin this next chapter and make friends. I was treading with my head slightly above water for the first time in motherhood sending one off to full day school, and felt like this was my opportunity to start new! But then I began to understand that she had her crew, and whether it was intentional or not, there wasn't room for one more. I've spent enough days wallowing in self-pity during motherhood, this was time for a braver, bigger-pantied Ashley to show up. I needed to create my own crew.

Hellbent on forging my own path, I put it out there to the few ladies that I had already met just by being outside, that I was going to host a wine night at my house.[2] I didn't even like wine at the time (gasp!), but it sounded like the adult thing to advertise and I was trying to make friends and impress these people *(I'm really more of a Bud Light or Tequila type girl)*. But for the sake of new friends, and casting the net wide enough to hopefully find at least one new friend, wine it was.

---

[2] Side note: in order to "find friends from just being outside", we need to put our phones away and actually be at the park with our heads up. That's neither here nor there, except for the fact that you don't look super friendly or open to new friends when you're just buried in your phone the whole time. Carry on. *steps off soap box*

We had just completed about 4.5 months of construction, and I figured if anything, people would come because we're all a bunch of lookie-loo's and their curiosity to the see the inside of the house that had been under construction all summer surely would at least get them in the door. I had met one other preschool mom in the area and asked her if she knew of any other moms who were in our stage of life. I made it a word of mouth, open invitation. Super informal – just come, bring a bottle of wine and we'll all get to know each other.

Oh my word, I was so nervous that first night. My palms were sweaty, I think I changed my shirt about four times, wanting to get it just right and make just the right impression. I couldn't look *too* put-together because I wanted to be real, but I also couldn't show *all* my gong show cards right out of the gates – the goal was to make friends here not scare them away! I was just looking to get to first base, that's it. About 30 minutes before people were supposed to show up, I got cold feet and immediately regretted my decision to send an open invite out to a bunch of strangers. This was dumb, no one was going to come! Let's just quit the party before I can be embarrassed that no one shows up. I always want to quit the party though. There is always a moment of doubt combined with a desire for self-preservation of my ego, to quit the party because it surely won't be as good as advertised, or cool enough with the right people, or whatever other dumb thought I allow to creep in. Which would be lamer: cancel the wine night 30 minutes before everyone was supposed to show, or leave it as is and have no one show up? I decided to place my chips on the latter, and put on my big girl panties to move forward with the night. After all, I was a sophisticated thirty-something now – in our twenties we would have quit the party, but this was my time to start fresh and start new, and frankly, grown-up new-to-the-neighborhood Ashley needed friends. Just one, that's all I was fishing for – just one!

Much to my surprise, at wine o'clock, the doorbell rang. Someone came! And to my surprise, she had brought a friend (*because you know how us ladies roll – we go in packs of two at minimum to new places; this is just girl code*). By the end of the evening, that very first wine night, there were 20 women who showed up. TWENTY!!! I literally knew three of them (and by *knew*, I mean, I had *met* four of them prior). I could cry just thinking about that first night. I had convinced myself that no one was going to show up, and nearly almost let my anxiety of the unknown shut the whole thing down. I didn't even know who the "who" would be. I just put it out there, and for whatever reason, people heard, and came.

Looking back, I just smile. We were all dying for connection. The oldest kid between all of us was in Kindergarten *(find your Kindergarten moms!!)*, and lived in the same neighborhood, but hadn't known each other. Someone needed to be vulnerable and willing to be known. Someone had to be the bridge and the connector. Or at least offer a place for people to connect. The desire amongst us all was there, but the environment hadn't been. And thankfully, in a moment of strength, I had dug deep and found the courage to say, "I'll go first." Everyone would ask as we were standing around my kitchen island, how do you know so-and-so and I would respond with I don't! I just met her tonight! I didn't know these people! We all were from various religious backgrounds, various cultural backgrounds, working moms, stay at home moms, IVF moms, preemie moms, step-moms. It didn't matter. They were all just like me; just a mom looking for some friends.

Now I realize that all of us don't live in these giant Leave-It-To-Beaver style neighborhoods where within walking distance, there's a small army of children and ~~zombies~~ moms to go with them. But we all have the capacity to make and be a friend. I've come to learn as we continue to age, and raise our kids, that there really is capacity for multiple circles and realms of friends. Friendships of proximity and convenience (aka neighborhood friends) are no less important than the friendships of the women who stood by you in your wedding. We need to collect them all. And oftentimes that requires us to be a big girl, and make the first move. Invite a new friend in. Start a wine night at your house. Initiate a play date with a neighbor mom. Stalk down that mom who you see walk by your house everyday (*I literally did this multiple times*)! Whatever it looks like, friendships will not happen unless you decide to make the first move. It requires courage and vulnerability, and some intentionality, but know and trust that all of us are craving that connection. You are not alone in your desire to be known on a deeper level and to have those people in your circle who can be your impromptu play-date or do-life-in-the-trenches people. The first step to those friendships is just simply that: a first step. A small invite. One act of vulnerability to say that you'll go first. And if for some reason your first invite falls flat on its face, keep at it. That's not an excuse to continue living in isolation and throw yourself a pity party. Life is better together in the trenches. Find your people. And hold on to them tightly.

CHAPTER 13

Unsolicited Advice

Jen Hatmaker writes about being the worst end of the school year mom ever. She summarizes all of me and my feelings about the end of the school year, but I could easily replace "school year" to "worst end of the summer mom ever". Because when you are a mom of little's, the summer is one of the most dreaded times. We're all excited come June for no schedules, no lunches *(which oh PS they still demand to eat lunch everyday*!), but then by August I am praying to the sweet baby Jesus for all of the teachers to put me out of my misery. They are just *there* at your house All. Day. Long. Every day, there they are. And yes, the sun is glorious and my kids spent countless hours running amuck outside, but when they are little little, the freedom to roam and wander isn't quite there yet. Summer consists of dumping sand out of their diapers and sweating within five minutes of being near any body of water because you're just trying to keep the littles from drowning themselves. Sunscreen on, lather, wash, repeat. There is not much that is relaxing about summer motherhood when there are littles under foot.

Before my middle guy "left" for Kindergarten *(despite my graphic wording, he just goes to the neighborhood public school, not a far away boarding school)*, I wanted to do something fun with him. With three kids, juggling multiple needs, multiple sets of emotions and schedules, I regularly parent in the masses. It's just too many voices talking to me all at once. My emotional status is more reminiscent of an IKEA kid table, than the parenting adult that is supposed to have authority over the chaos. So I decided I wanted some one on one time and scheduled some fun *(remember, we schedule fun? – this is what we do when we're running a gong show)*. The qualifications for me to regain emotional stability meant we needed to get on a plane and leave the everyday behind - hello Vacation Mom! So with my husband's approval (he saw my state of emotional distress) I planned a top secret, last minute, trip to the mecca of all kid locales: Disneyland. Not only were we going to the Motherland of magicalness and churros, but I was only taking one kid in tow. Yep, you read that right: one kid. And before you go assuming that Disneyland is a regular destination for our family, it is not. None of us (minus me from when I was a wee one) had ever been. Not even our oldest kid. Gasp! I know, that's how unstable my end of the summer emotional status was. I took one kid, and not the others, despite the fact that they had never been either.

I was so excited for this trip and to get in this precious time with just my one kid that I didn't anticipate all of the crap I would get from others when I told them of my grand plans. *You're only taking one kid? Won't your oldest be so mad? How is he going to feel? Shouldn't you at least take both older kids so that it's fair?* I began to doubt my grand plans as magical, and second-guessed everything. *Was I making a decision that would ruin my other kids by taking just one to Disneyland and not the others? Should I simultaneously be adding to their counseling account for this trip because of sibling jealousy?* For real, I began to believe the words of others against what I knew to be the right thing for our family in my heart, and nearly cancelled my trip. Thank the Lord though for the more rational half of me (aka my husband), because with his reassurance (the brain of a man doesn't give two effs about irrational sibling equality), I didn't cancel the trip and stuck with the original plan to just take one. I pushed through the doubt and overwhelming outside judgement from others, and knew that what my mama heart needed at the end of that grueling summer was a couple of days with just my middle man.

The two days at Disney were *exactly* what my mama heart had needed. It was every bit as magical as you would imagine, complete with churros and ice cream after nearly every meal. Separating the one from the masses allowed me to see this little boy for who he was and really relish in the gift that he is to our family. For 48 hours, he got all of me and me all of him. I don't remember specifics of what we talked about, and I'm sure none of it was ground-breaking, but I will *always* remember the feeling that I had just being able to be with him. I am so thankful that I didn't listen, or give any ground to the voices of others who were telling me that this magical plan of mine wasn't right, or wasn't fair, and that I shouldn't go.

One of the realities of life is simply that others *will* attempt to stomp out your plans. I'm not sure why we as moms do this to each other. I mostly think it's unintentional. We're bad listeners, and we're not super good at celebrating others. Inadvertently, by running our own mouths and sharing our opinions, we might be squashing someone else's dreams. I almost listened to the judgmental cautions from older, wiser moms, who warned me against taking one kid and not the other. But the reality is, I know my kids best. And you know YOUR kids best. What works for my family, might not work for yours. But if one mom is dreaming up a victory with her kid, let's celebrate that rather than squash it. When we choose collaboration over competition, everyone wins.

For me, in that season, going to Disneyland with just one kid was what seemed fun. I needed to laugh with my kid and enjoy him. I needed to not parent in the masses and get out of the long hot days of summer. People told me it was a terrible idea. I had tears of guilt. I couldn't sleep the entire night before the trip, riddled with guilt.

Going so far as looking up a last minute flight for my other kids just to make it fair. But the only reason I was doing those things, was because a few others had given me their unsolicited advice. Don't make decisions based on other people's projected guilt. What a gift that trip was. Literally, one of my all-time favorite memories. I can't say that up until this point, I've had a ton of memorable REALLY good days as a mom. It's been hard. But this trip, one that I almost didn't take because of mom guilt, goes down in the record books as one of the best ever. We had SO much fun.

I can't parent based on other people's opinions, or their ideas of what's fair or unfair. One of my favorite authors always says, "Other people's opinions of you are none of your business"[3], or in other words: let other people's opinions of you and how you are choosing to show up for motherhood in that moment go in one ear and out the other. Fairness and equality are two different things in our household. We love each kid equally, and also uniquely. Honestly, I was prepared for so much heat and backlash from the other kids for not taking them to Disney, but there was literally zero. None. I'm not 100% sure why that was the case, but I can speculate that it's because our kids know and trust that I'm going to show up for them in the best way possible each and every time. They trust their time will come. And frankly, it will, and has. You as the mama get to be the owner of how your house runs – other people's opinions hold zero

[3] Rachel Hollis

weight when it comes to doing what's best for your mama heart.

Even small adventures with one kid helps to provide the perspective you need to pull yourself out of the weeds of parenting in the masses, and see your kid as a gift instead of the terdburger he's acting like with all of his siblings. Take just one to the grocery store. Throw one of the littles into the back of your car to the post office. Mundane everyday car rides become holy ground for conversations when you only have one kid in the car. Plus, where else can you strap in your child and have their undivided attention? My point is that separating one of your kiddos from the rest will not only fill their tank, but sometimes more importantly, fill *your* tank. There is no guilt to be had, there are no fairness rules on how and when you can spend individual time with your kids. No one gets to be the boss of how you run your household other than you *(and your partner)*. So stop weighing other people's opinions on how you should and should not parent into the weight of your daily decisions. You can be confident in the tools that you have to make the decisions that are best for your family, leaving mom guilt where it belongs – in the weekly trash.

CHAPTER 14

The Easy Button

Our dreams as women oftentimes can be some of the most intimate thoughts that we possess. As little girls in our generation, we were told and encouraged to be anything that we want to be. But little by little, as you grow up, the world pokes holes in that theology and ideology. Life has gotten in the way, or thrown you a few curve balls and handed you a few insecurities. When I was little, I vividly remember sitting in front of the TV one morning probably with my breakfast in my lap because I am a product of the 80s, watching an episode of Oprah. She was interviewing various professionals for them to talk about their jobs and career choices. And she interviewed an OBGYN, which was A LOT of letters and sounded REALLY fancy *(which naturally piqued my interest for a career of assumed prestige)* and translated his fancy job title to "a baby doctor". In my head, what I heard him say was, "I get to hold little babies and make lots of money all day." So from there on, I would proudly declare to any wondering adult who always asks the inevitable question to every unassuming child, "What do you want to be when you grow up?" And I would shoot back without hesitation, "an OBGYN." I held this career aspiration for many years, and I'd regurgitate my fancy baby doctor goals to any teacher or friend who asked. It wasn't until 8th grade that we did a career unit in school, that I began to understand that to be an OBGYN, my days might be filled with a bit more than just holding babies all day. Like for example, I most likely would be staring at and touching lots of vaginas all day. And that I would from here on out, need to be taking primarily ALL science classes. And not like potions and motions, but like the really really hard sciences. And YES, I would most likely receive a sizable paycheck someday for my efforts but it would only come after years and YEARS of EXTRA school (which to say to a pubescent eighth grader might as well be a death sentence). Yeah, no - I'm out. Suddenly, my "drive" to be a baby doctor someday went quickly down the drain. It wasn't what I thought it was going to be, and I could see that a life of vaginas and lots of school sounded like an opportune time to take a right-hand turn right *off* that career track.

Maybe what you thought your dream would be, isn't really all that it's cracked up to be and you are left feeling deep-rooted feelings of discontent. Or maybe now as you've entered the world of being a mom, your dreams may feel like they're on hold or have gone by the wayside. There's no longer room for you. You are no longer the main character in your own life, but instead have been reduced to a footnote in the acknowledgement section toward the back of the book. I get it. I feel all those things on the regular too.

Even though I wished so deeply to be a mom, I found myself wishing away the days as soon as it became hard. I would see those Staples commercials with the big red, "Easy" buttons and dream of a world where I could order one and put it next to my bedside table for when things got hard. Really, this Easy Button was an Escape Button. We should re-brand it with a palm tree because that's how I wanted to use it. I just wanted to escape. I'd wake up from a less-than restless night's sleep to immediate sibling squabbles, or crying, or an unexpected fever from a little, that would thwart my entire days' worth of plans, and just think *anywhere but here today God; anyone but me.*

With the birth of our oldest, my heart just felt like it was going to explode and burst at any given moment because I just never knew that I could love in that manner. But as soon as those feelings wore off, and we kept adding more babies, the realities of my daily life looked a hell of a lot different than the gold-framed Hallmark movie I had envisioned in my brain. I would cry to my husband, or friends, or in the shower constantly, daily, living in the tension of feeling like this is what I dreamt of and asked for, so why does it feel so hard? Why do I feel like this is such a burden? These kids are getting in the way of my life! And then quickly, escapism would set in again, and my dreams shifted. I'd spend mindless hours dreaming up a life that surely would satisfy. I figured I could trade in my motherhood dreams *(since clearly this wasn't what I thought it was going to be and wasn't delivering great results all around)*, or what it was cracked up to be, and exchange them for a better life toward career and purpose dreams. I would long for the days when fevers and sibling squabbles are but a distant memory. I would think, "Once I get past these child-rearing years, then I can *really* get to the good stuff and live out my purpose." I just couldn't understand why if I had so clearly felt like I was meant to be a mom, and so clearly felt that the choice to stay home with them full time was exactly the thing that I needed to be doing for our family, why was it coming up so short in the fulfillment bank? Why was it so freaking hard?

Sometimes our dreams look different than our reality, even when they are realized. Sometimes our dreams fall short of expectation. We dream with our rose-colored glasses on, *(but we only realize that in hindsight)*, but when we come to the arrival point and look around, we realize we're not exactly in the land of milk and honey. Gold-paved streets aren't in this neighborhood. The more that we put our hope in our circumstances, the less fulfilling our everyday is going to feel. Our circumstances are so temporary, that when we put our hope in "someday", we will always arrive at someday feeling less than fulfilled. Someday will never be the thing that brings us purpose and contentment. I am a huge fan of reaching, and running hard after your dreams, whatever they may look like, but I can promise you that the more that you put your hope, and identity, in the fulfillment and realization of that dream, the emptier it's going to feel when you get there. There is no job, no role, no title, no vacation or status level that will give you that feeling of contentment we all crave. Those are *things* and should not be the basis for our hope. I once heard it said from a former NFL player who had been to the Superbowl (and won!), that Jesus is better than the Superbowl.[4] If the freaking Superbowl, which is the dream of all dreams for men, can't even bring that lasting joy we crave, then we need to trade out our dreams and goals for something that will actually last and fulfill. We need a perspective shift. We need to stop chasing after our dreams to give us joy, and start chasing after the thing, or more specifically the person, that claims to be the giver of joy and purpose. For me, that has been Jesus.

In the book of Psalms, the author of the book, David says, "Delight yourself in the Lord and he will grant the desires of your heart"[5]. What I found to be true in my own journey, was that the more that I looked to Jesus in the everyday, the softer my heart grew toward my kids and my role as a mom. I ever-so-slowly began to watch the desires of my heart change. Would a new career really be the thing that brought me joy? Would a vacation or getaway – an actual escape – really be the

---

[4] *Becoming*, Clint Gresham

[5] Psalm 37:4

143

thing that filled my cup to then come back and love my family well? Maybe. But those circumstances were temporary. I needed to learn how to lean in when things got hard and not just immediately reach for that Easy Button. Motherhood is gritty. Every day is a freaking GRIND sometimes. As I write this, we are sitting dead center in the middle of a global pandemic, and I've been quarantined with my kids for 30 days...and counting. Trust me, an Easy Button sounds like HEAVEN right now. But this job, this journey, this role of Mom does not come with an Easy Button. But I've learned that I have more grit and determination than I thought. Sometimes, I have to remind myself that I'm the adult and I will prevail. I roll up my sleeves and tell those terdburgers what's up. Other days, grit looks like scratching your day's agenda just to cuddle and play ten rounds of Crazy 8s. It's merely about balance. []

If motherhood wasn't your dream job, or isn't your dream job as your everyday 9-5, I see you. I wholeheartedly believe our dreams are put in our hearts for a reason – you don't feel the tension of the struggle for no reason, it is not in vain. Work toward them, put pen to paper and work toward making it happen, but know that your hope cannot be in these dreams as the thing that will bring you purpose. There is no amount of achieving OUT THERE (in the world) that will supersede or be more important, than serving your family in here. I had to make the conscious choice to lay down my dreams of prestige, success, and impact through a career outside of the home for now, because for eight years, my method wasn't working. And oh how I wish I could say that I've come out the other side with all of the answers, the biggest one being the formula for how to be content in my job as a mom. But the reality is that it's a process. If I want my heart's desires to match my circumstances, I must pour it out to Jesus – the giver of peace and joy and purpose - everyday, and continue to show up trusting that I've been given that dream for a reason, but I might just be in a season of not yet. And that's okay for today. I'll continue to serve whoever is right in front of me. And trust that this is where I'm supposed to show up today. And we'll deal with tomorrow when tomorrow comes.

CHAPTER 15

Open Doors

One day, probably right in the middle of cleaning up lunch time crumbs or sitting down comfortably for the first time to turn on some reality TV during nap time, I saw a random area code come across my phone. Out of sheer boredom *(and a bit of curiosity)* in my everyday life, I decided to answer. It was a lady whom I had never met before, offering me an opportunity to join together with some other women and come down for a two-day focus group in Santa Barbara, CA. Accommodations and food were covered, I just needed to get myself there. I didn't hear anything she had to say about why, or where she even got my name and number, all I heard was two days away from my kids in California! Without even consulting my husband, I asked where did I need to sign on the dotted line because I was IN.

With my sunglasses in hand, completely blind as to why I was invited or even there, but simply just wanting to get away, I booked a ticket blindly to wine country and went on that trip. To my surprise, what I ended up finding was something that absolutely lit my soul on fire in ways that I honestly never really had unlocked before. I say unlocked because I believe that these things, these passions, already exist inside of you. The glimmers of life you see come out of you or the way your ears perk up or heart starts to burn when someone begins talking about things that fire you up. They were put there on purpose, you just sometimes have to mine them out because they get buried in the monotony of life. They can especially get *real* buried in the years of raising and caring for little people, when demand every ounce of your physical and emotional being is in demand. I digress.

Upon arrival, I walked into an outdoor space of strangers. After just having flown for two hours without my children though, my eyes and heart were wide open – I was on vacation! Multiple generations of women were gathered from all over to the country talking about two things that I knew I cared about: generosity and women. I did *not* know though that these two subjects would lead me to feeling more purpose than I had felt since becoming a mom. This fire within had been buried beneath the monotony of motherhood. It didn't matter how I got invited into the conversation, the only thing that mattered was that I was there, and my voice needed to be heard because I apparently had things to say. Little by little, throughout my two days with these women, I began to feel like myself again. Confidence began to grow as the inner fire and passion inside of me began to emerge. There were tiny bits of confidence in me that I hadn't felt or seen in a while. The shell began to crack open and I began to hear my voice again and get excited – and even better, trust it. I began to engage in the conversation around women and generosity in ways that I had never considered before. I read the book, _When Women Give_ by Kim King and she rocked my world with statistics about the wealth of America and how over two-thirds of it will be in the hands and control of women within the next 30 years. These were some big numbers and some really big ideas and I knew I wanted to include my friends in this conversation. I knew that they needed to be a part of the movement to find freedom in our everyday lives through _money_, and I knew this maybe would light their souls on fire the way it had mine. The best part was that the only prerequisite to be a part of the movement was to simply show up with the little you had. No millionaires, trust funds, or inheritance accounts needed – it was called a giving circle, and I wanted to start one at home with my people. I could see, and feel, that this was a means toward freedom not just for me, but for my friends.

Maybe you've heard of giving circles, or maybe you haven't. But for the sake of an even playing field, basically the simple concept of a giving circle is a set amount of money is pre-determined and required for each person to bring to the table _(in our case, everyone invited needed to bring $100)_, the hosts present three worthy causes or non-proft organizations, they make a very brief proposal for how people's collective donation would be used, then as a group a winner is voted upon. Each person making a donation has a vote, the majority wins, and the individual donations get pooled together to present one giant lump sum of money toward the winning initiative. Within an hour or so, we'd make a big donation to that worthy cause and walk away from a super purposeful girls night not only receiving a ton of connection with friends, but also making a difference in our community. Easy peasy – this was a no brainer for me. Super simple – you show up with $100, drink a glass of wine, hang out with your girlfriends, and by the end of the night, as a group, we'll have made a $5,000-$10,000 donation to an organization or cause that really needed it. The best part was that it was a no-frills event. No extensive décor or planning were required as is traditionally needed with fundraisers in the past. This was more of a guerilla boots-on-the-ground type effort that most any mom could attend, and even plan, as long as they felt passionate about extending the invite to their network of friends. I figured that wine and girls night were enough to get my neighbors and friends out, because well KIDS AT HOME, so onward into initiating hosting my first ever Giving Circle.

The night was a huge success. Women from all over our city came, each bringing a friend or two with them, and we walked away making a giant impact for an inner-city youth program right in our own backyard. There were no frills, no super exclusive invite list, you didn't even have to wear SPANX or curl your hair. We simply gathered for a purpose. It was like magic too! I had never

considered making a $10,000 donation on my own –
that would be a GIANT deal in our household, and one
that both Blake and I would vet and weigh out heavily
most likely for MONTHS. But $100 to a good cause?
That feels way more doable in our household. And all I
had to do was say WINE NIGHT, and women were in.

What's funny is that all of a sudden, after the Giving
Circle, I started caring about inner-city youth. I wanted
to know where my money was going, I wanted to know
who these kids were that were about to receive close to
$10,000 from our group. I followed that curiosity and it
led me to begin a relationship with Jasmine, the staffer
who works with the inner-city kids. It's really not
surprising that I started caring, because Jesus said that
where my money is, my heart will follow, and that's
exactly what happened. Suddenly, I cared about inner
city kids and I cared about how they were being
provided for, and wanted to get more involved and help
connect other women who maybe had additional
resources that could help too. I started calling Jasmine
and asking how the kids were. I wanted to know if they
needed shampoo or conditioner, or if there were other
ways that we could rally around these kids. This was not
a hand out, we wanted genuine relationship to form for a
hand up. Not because it's my job as a white woman to
save the world but rather because my heart was being
transformed and rallying around the kids in our very
own backyard was a natural outpouring. My heart
toward this group of seemingly strangers was expanding
and growing, even in the midst of being knee-deep in

raising and caring for my own kids. More space was being added in my day to day for the thing that I never knew I needed to care about. I started learning about poverty culture, white privilege, and white fragility, and immersing myself in a world that I hadn't previously been exposed to *(or chosen to be exposed to)*. A passion was growing inside of me simply because I kept saying yes to one invitation forward after another. I did not know when I answered a random California area code instead of pressing play to *Keeping Up With the Kardashian (yes, I really do watch that show. QUIT your judgement Karen)* that one year later I'd be hosting a girl's night, standing in front of 75 women asking them to give $100 to help inner city youth – those dots were so far from each other and something that I never could have connected. But saying yes to the first open door was exactly how I began to unlock the connection toward purpose. My relationship with Jasmine has continued to grow. I purposefully left the door open with her, long after the big check from our Giving Circle arrived.

Where my money is, there my heart is also. I care about the things where my money goes toward. This is also true for less noble things. I spend a lot of money on my hair and clothes...and guess what I care a ton about? My appearance. *(the vanity streak of an Enneagram three is ROUGH on my checkbook)* I guarantee that if you take a look at your checkbook, you will be able to see what your heart cares about. Or maybe a better way to say it is your checkbook will be the real-life tale of exactly what what you *say* you care about versus what you *actually* care about. That's not a judgement, but rather a challenge. One that I continually use for myself and our family. Are our values reflected in our bank statements? Or maybe you're already very on board for this, and you're ignoring the passions and causes and purposes you already have and serve! Show me your checkbook, and I will show you what you care about. Because as Chris Tucker once said, *Money Talks*.

CHAPTER 16

Find Your People – Sister Wives, To Be Clear

The newfound freedom from rediscovering and reclaiming my identity inside and outside of motherhood has left me in a funny season of life. I no longer care to impress, care to fit in with the stereotype, or care to try to pretend that just because I may have the *time available* to help in the classroom, does not mean that I want to. But I will hang out with my friends and do other activities all day long.

Our neighborhood hosts an annual Easter Egg hunt in the park behind our house every year. The previous owners of our house told us one of the conditions of us purchasing this home was that we needed to commit to continuing to see the Egg Hunt tradition through for years to come – they had started it, and tradition should live on. The hunt is exactly how you'd imagine it to be, complete with a high-schooler dressed as an Easter bunny, kid bike parade usually led by an Abe Lincoln or two on motorcycles, donuts, and enough eggs to fill the state fair's chicken hut. That first year in our house, I volunteered to be Ground Zero for the egg hunt, starting with inviting all of my neighborhood mom friends over to stuff thousands of eggs a few nights before the event. Everyone brought a bottle of wine to share, we dumped out the candy, each had a giant bin of eggs to fill, and we began our egg stuffing assembly line. We were such devoted mothers *sacrificing* our time for the sake of the children we bore. Orrrrrrr....we just all really wanted a girls night. Now after approximately 10 bins were filled with eggs, our stamina for the beloved project was waning, the Pinot & Cabernet were starting to kick in, and we were becoming more and more interested in simply chatting and hanging out. Except there were still hundreds of eggs to be stuffed.

We had ourselves a dilemma: the children needed the eggs, but the workers were fading quickly.

Perfectionism went out the window with the third kid, so my philosophy hovers more around just get the job done. Done is better than perfect. If we need to cut a few corners, no big deal. Afterall, we're the #okayest at these sorts of things. It started to become quite clear that none of said workers were ever really primarily interested in egg stuffing or curating a perfect event for the children, we just needed an excuse to chat and hang out. In an attempt to "finish", we made a mad scramble to rid the table with all remaining candy and stuffed treasures into whatever egg was nearest, and then brashly throw them in a bin to call it good. Methods of sufficiency and systems for coordinating stuffing prizes with matching age groups and labeled bins were thrown out the window in the name of mom's night in. The desire for community and connection trumped any magically curated childhood event.

Fast forward to the day of the egg hunt, when we received an unsolicited response from a neighbor (*whom had not been in attendance to the egg stuffing extravaganza*), noting that her child was so excited to have received an entire roll of stickers in his egg. She praised the homeowners for the generosity of prizes this year and was pleased with the upgrade in loot.

Whoopsiedoodle.

At some point during the rush to just "finish the job", someone had thought it appropriate that instead of tearing off individual stickers for each egg, that the faster way to finish was to simply throw the entire roll in one egg. Done.

I died.

I knew these were my people. Done is better than perfect, and sometimes done is even better than right. Good enough for our kids is actually good enough. Parenting philosophy of champions; put it in your back pocket for the next project – that nugget is a free gift with purchase for you.

But finding friends in your late twenties, thirties, and even forties is an entirely different beast. People have careers now, oftentimes 2.5 children in tow, and it's not like you're frequenting the clubs *(I never frequented the clubs, let's be honest)* or the dorms. Finding your people in the deep end of raising kids is hard. I hear you, let's talk about it.

One of my most favorite guilty pleasures while folding laundry is binge-watching episodes of TLC's Sister Wives. I am just fascinated by this family, and how they have chosen to structure things. Four wives, one husband and a gaggle of kids, all doing life together (literally) in one cul de sac. There have been many days where I look at the small village that they have created in their parent-rearing structure and think, yes, I can see the benefit to that! But since I am unwilling to share my husband, this has never been a legit option.

Instead of raising our kids with four moms, or in a village as our ancestors once did, parenting has become a thing of isolation. In a recent study conducted by

CIGNA, it was reported that today most Americans are reportedly at the highest rates of loneliness in history. In an age where we are virtually connected to anyone and everyone, twenty-four hours a day, we are the loneliest we've ever been. The study shows that one in four Americans rarely or never feel as though there are people who really understand them. And two in five Americans reported that their relationships are not meaningful and that they are isolated from others[6]. As staggering as these statistics are, they don't shock me. Our culture is very much "me-centric", where all of the advertising and marketing is geared toward encouraging us to believe that if we only get this certain gadget, or work our way to a certain income level, or gain access to a particular product, that we will receive the golden carrot: happiness and contentment. It is a promise sold to us by every advertiser in America that is completely false. Their entire job is to sell you a lifestyle through their product. And yet we fall for it, multiple times a day, without even consciously being aware. And the result is that we are left feeling empty and lonely, or eventually exhausted because we've been running and chasing an ideal for so long, and it never satisfies.

We were created for community and connection. If the average American is reporting meaningless relationships and deep-rooted feelings of loneliness and isolation, how much greater are those feelings magnified

[6] https://www.cigna.com/about-us/newsroom/studies-and-reports/loneliness-epidemic-america

for the mom next door who spends her days physically caring for the tiny army she has created, with little to no meaningful connection? I remember so clearly when my kids were super little, before preschool and before elementary school, my life and schedule revolved around nap times and playdates. Our days were totally structured around when the little ones would (*hopefully*) sleep. Morning nap, playdate, lunch time, afternoon nap, maybe another playdate, dinner time, followed by bed time – we lived and breathed around when they ate and slept. Occasionally at one of these playdates, I maybe might get in a full sentence with the other adult we were "playing" with, but most likely the entire playdate was spent keeping the children from killing themselves and/or making sure they didn't put more garbage off the ground in their mouth and choke. It is a season of pure physical and emotional exhaustion, which in my opinion only adds to the loneliness we already feel. And that's not even factoring in trauma in your pregnancy, trauma in your delivery, sick kids, special needs, and a million other factors that may make us feel outside of the realm of "normal" motherhood. Like we don't fit in and don't have a place.

Based on the statistics though, it's a wonder why more women aren't talking about this loneliness. Because it all came as a surprise to me. No wonder I had post baby blues! All I would crave everyday was a meaningful conversation; from someone that didn't need anything from me. Or whose butt I didn't need to wipe. And I quickly realized that something had to change. I'd walk the neighborhood during the day, and I would be the only living soul I would see. Where were all the people? Working? Maybe. Holed up in their house too? Probably. Occasionally, a grey-haired being walking their dog, but for the most part, the "community" wasn't actually very communal. Our first home with babies was in a neighborhood in the suburbs because that's where they told me all the people would be, but it didn't feel very neighborly. The garage doors would open and the cars would quickly pull in and shut the door before we could say hi. Or I'd find myself at the park surrounded by little people who could easily make friends with my little people, but the adults responsible for watching them were all the nannies. Me and the nannies hanging out. Nannies are wonderful, and working outside of the home moms are SO necessary and I'm such a cheerleader for women in the workplace, but for whatever reason, that wasn't the season I was called to be in for my family at the time. And thus, my circles looked like me and a bunch of millennials who were lovely, but definitely not my people. Where were my sister wives? Where were the other women of the village that were supposed to be there in the trenches with me, linking arms and doing this thing together? I craved connection and meaning in small and big ways. And I could see that if I didn't carve out the time to make it happen, it wasn't just going to spontaneously occur. That's just not how our culture and society live anymore. I had to go searching for it.

I've always encouraged new moms to find a pregnancy partner. That sounds weird, I know. This is someone who you will have an ongoing text strand with, that dings all hours of the night, as you walk the journey of motherhood together. Each stage. The painful Charlie horses during pregnancy. The growing waistline. The constipation. The middle of the night cravings for absurd things. The fears of labor and delivery (*do you think we really will poop during it??*). This partner in crime will get you in ways that your actual partner won't. She will be a lifeline to you when literal, and metaphorical, shit hits the fan. The one that you can confide in who understands your journey in a way that only someone walking that same path would. She brings solidarity and sanity to your feelings of insecurity, insanity, and loneliness.

She is for lack of a better term, your sister wife.

For me, that partner was my best friend, Kendra. We had our first-born babes seven months a part, and then popped out our second-borns five weeks apart, and our third-borns were in the hospital together at the same time, only seven days apart (*mine was a NICU baby but that's a story for another time and place*). Having Kendra walk this road side by side with me has been one of the most meaningful relationships and connections in my life. Because not only do you start as pregnancy partners, but then it evolves into playdate partners, getaway partners, toddler partners, and on and on into each parenting stage. We weren't ever the ones physically helping one another. Nope, I loved her too much to ask her to take my kids. I knew that her gong show everyday was just as bad as mine. We joke that even though we had babies at the same time, we never held each other's babies because neither one of us had the capacity to give one more ounce of care for another tiny human at the time. But she was there in the middle of the night. She was there when I felt misunderstood by my husband. She was there when I felt lost as a mom. She was there when I needed someone to remind me that I *was* actually more than a mom.

We cannot do this motherhood thing alone. Fine, being an actual sister wife feels a bit extreme, but living in a commune doesn't sound all that bad when you're in the trenches every single day. Simply having that connection breathes life into the hard days like nothing else can. I believe that this is how we were wired. We were meant to be in community, and meant to help carry the load of one another. Even if it's just emotional. Doesn't have to be physical – it might just look like an ongoing text strand with someone who gets you. Everyone needs a sister wife.

Eventually Kendra and I each got to a breaking point after our second kids were born, where we were craving connection beyond just the regular run of the mill playdate circuit. The loneliness factor was growing like a scoby in kombucha *(really showing my Seattle roots there)*, as the needs of the little's began to wear on us. We began implementing Freedom Fridays. It started as a joke when one day the stars aligned and each of us discovered that we both had made childcare arrangements that happened to align with each other on a Friday. One Friday became two Fridays became three Fridays, and before we knew it, this has become a thing. Freedom Fridays quickly turned into the most beloved day of our entire week. I realized that we *needed* these Fridays. Some days would be made up of frivolous window shopping and manicures and other days would look like simply sharing a good meal, having uninterrupted conversation and pouring out our hearts to one another. Talking about what was really happening in our households behind closed doors. Sharing the last ten percent with another human. It quickly became a very sacred time. And for some reason (God bless our husbands) us each prioritizing the time and recognizing the benefit somehow relieved any mom guilt that we may have felt at the time because I had a partner in crime who was doing the same thing with her family. I *knew* this was good for my soul, and having a friend doing it with me was the exact permission that I needed to gift myself this time free of guilt.

Pulling back the curtain and revealing our true selves can be scary. Don't trust that privilege with just anyone. The innermost parts of you are sacred and vulnerable, and don't need to be given to just anyone. In time, this place in your life will be earned. But don't fear going there first. Find your person, or if you're lucky, people, and risk being vulnerable. Risk going there in search of connection. When we let someone in, give them a peak under the hood, that is when the loneliness starts to fade. Connection becomes our antidote to the loneliness.

Somewhere along the line, us women have sold ourselves short on the importance of prioritizing self-care. This is stupid. We feel inadequate, not worth it, or that it is our duty to simply endure the hard (*for me*) little years. I'm not sure where that messaging started, but nowhere else in the land of the working human, have I found a job that requires you to be on duty and on call twenty-four seven, three hundred and sixty-five days a week. If someone were to tell you that was their work schedule and that they regularly went without sick and vacation leave, you would think they had purchased a one-way ticket to burn-out city. And for me, I was on that fast track quicker than Joanna Gaines could complete an episode of Fixer Upper. Freedom Fridays were my ticket off the train. I needed off. I needed connection. And I was worth it.

As we have continued to make friends along the way, Freedom Fridays have stayed at the forefront of our time for connection. They are no longer a weekly habit for Kendra and I that we partake in regularly (*we don't even live in the same city sadly anymore*), but they are still an internal value in how we structure our family, and personally how I structure the juggle of work and motherhood. Just because you are a mom does not mean that you don't need, or deserve, time off. And just because you don't earn a paycheck, does not mean that you don't need, or deserve, regular and consistent time off. Let me be the first to give you permission that it is okay for you to take time out for yourself. Do not wait until the one day a year on Mother's Day to gift yourself permission to stop and just not do anything. That is not only a disservice to you, but also to the people around you. It is good and right to rest on the regular. We cannot wait until we're at the point of burn out when the match has already been lit to burn the whole thing down. Establishing a regular and consistent rhythm of rest is literally one of the best ways you can love yourself and your people. Rest is essential in motherhood if you plan to make it to the end of this road with your sanity and self still in tact. I am a better mom when I have regular breaks. I am a better wife when I have scheduled time for myself. And that time is not spent just doing frivolous things. Sometimes yes, but most of the time no! I want my soul to be recharged and I want to be intentional with my time off. I am involved in local organizations, I volunteer (*NOT in the classroom – I love you teachers!*), I blog, I grocery shop, and meal plan. I spend time not just focused on me, but on things that I know will help me grow. I'm tired of women discounting themselves and their roles as moms. I'm tired of culture sending the message that as moms it is our job to be martyrs in our homes and let go of all the things that make us whole. Enough! It is a privilege and honor to be raising the next generation, but that does not mean that it isn't hard or worthwhile. You need a break, just the same as the CEO next door. I have friends who have gone so far as to implement a formal vacation policy for the mom in their household, just as she would receive in a job outside of the home.

To gift ourselves rest in the everyday is to love our people well. It is honestly less about the *how*, but more about the *who*. You, my friend, are worth it. Yes, even as an unpaid mom in the home. Yes, even as a full-time career outside of the home mom who feels like she doesn't spend enough time with her kids. Yep, you still deserve rest too. We need to be okay caring for ourselves in the same way that we care for everyone else around us. It is not written anywhere that says to be a good mom means that you have to sacrifice yourself for 18 years. Nope. I'm not to the end of my kids-at-home 24/7 motherhood journey and I am nowhere near launching children into the world, but I can only imagine the identity crisis that will come if I spend 18 years caring for others without honoring me in the process. It doesn't have to be one or the other, we can do both. And in fact, dare I say it is *good* and *right* to do both.

CHAPTER 17

Dressing for the Job

Alright ladies, let's talk for a few minutes about our wardrobes. One of the best things ever introduced into the mom-world was the trend of Athleisure, because Lord knows I love me some stretchy, high-waisted, comfy pants just as much as the next girl. We can even take a moment of pause for elastic in the waistbands. Thank you Lord, this is how I know you love me. But where I draw the line is living and dressing like an absolute slob kebob just because you are a mom.

Now look, I have been in the pickup and drop off line a million times, dressed like I just rolled out of bed with no bra, because let's face it, there's a good chance that was true. But if you want to be taken seriously as a mom professional, whether you work inside or outside of the home, and break the glass ceiling of gender stereotypes we've been oppressed by in our culture for far too long, then you need to start dressing like the CEO that you are. This might require a slight mindset shift to begin viewing yourself as the actual BOSS that you really are. I don't care what your office looks like – whether it's inside the home with no paycheck, or outside of the home with a ballin' paycheck – you are a boss! I'm not saying you need a million-dollar line item for clothing in your budget - that's absurd - but I am saying that you need to wear clothes that fit your current body, and sometimes that is going to require a few dollars.

My body yo-yoed just like the rest of you with each baby that I carried. At 5'7", I gained 60 pounds my first go-round. I lived on a permanent diet of boxed mashed potatoes and Ivar's takeout. Gross. I don't even know how I gained so much weight *(other than when I think about how many Eggnog Milkshakes I may have consumed)* because I was SO sick. I was sick until almost 30 weeks. Princess Kate lost a ton of weight and got checked in to a hospital. Me? I was sick and still managed to gain more weight than a beluga whale. When I got to the point where my weight had surpassed that of my husband's, and even his clothes no longer fit me, I decided that had been enough. With each kid, and each season up....and each season back down, my body went through just as many sizes. But it was an important part of my recovery, both with adjusting to a new baby and battling post-partum, to feel good about myself. Clothes were one tiny way for me to control this. The days when I was wearing sweats that were five sizes too big, or squeezing into jeans that were five sizes too small, I just felt defeated and like crap. Granted, I didn't give enough credit to the number of hormones that were flooding my post-partum body, but there were some things that I could control that began to effect, and change, the way I felt. The gift of a shower to myself everyday was one of those. Now, look, these are not hard and fast rules, and there is no measure of perfection – like I've created some sort of checklist every day that you must complete in order to be a good mom. No! On the contrary, these are suggestions to HELP and grace can oftentimes be the best checklist you write for the day. Sick kid? Yeah, showers might get punted for a few days. So please hear me when I say that this is not a formula or recipe for success, but rather tools to put in your toolbelt for the times when you DO carve out the margin in your day for yourself. You're going to have to prioritize it because it won't ever just magically COME to you. But I recognize that motherhood has the magic of the unknown and unexpected, so the more we can flex with our days and circumstances in the hard times, the better off we'll be.

I know that we each have that pair of "goal jeans" or goal whatever's, in our closet, and my advice for you on those is a lot like Elsa's: LET IT GO. There are companies and services out there now whose sole job is to help you look and feel good. Clothes make a difference. It sounds stupid and shallow, but imagine if a female CEO showed up to an all-male board room meeting to make a presentation wearing her college sweats and a spit-up stained tee shirt? They'd laugh. No one would take her seriously – including HER. In the same vein, let's start applying that to our jobs at home. We need to start showing up as the person that we want to be, and that includes our personal appearance. Go to the drug store and buy a cute nail color for $2.99, come home, turn on a show or a podcast and take a few minutes to paint your freaking nails. They don't have to be perfect – your skills will increase with time. But it's one tiny act of rebellion that will help your mindset begin to shift toward feeling better about you, and the job that you are doing at home. After I had my third baby, my house could be on fire *(actually the fire most likely would be something in the kitchen)*, the kids could be screaming, the baby could be crying but as long as my nails were done, I was feeling like I had at least some of my shit together, and that was enough to power me through. I could look down in the middle of my 4,000th load of dishes for the day and see a cute bright color peaking back at me, reminding me that yes, I was once a person who existed outside of these four walls.

Self-care is not selfish. And we tend to poo-poo it as frivolous or shallow. And yes, if your motivation becomes simply to look good, then that's one thing. But I don't believe that about you. Investing in yourself, investing in your wardrobe *(at EACH phase of your body)*, treating yourself to a bath bomb or extended stay shower will do wonders for your mental health and self-esteem. Let go of the guilt that getting your hair done, or painting your nails, is something that only the vain participate in. Hogwash. Caring for yourself is one of the best gifts you can give to your family. Showing them that Mommy means business. Showing them that you are showing up to work every day, just the same as you expect them to be showing up for their jobs *(there's not enough space in this book to tackle kid school clothes wars – I quit on that front)*. Set the tone for your day. Get up, shower and show up for work. Call on companies and women like Evereve or Stitch Fix to help you in seasons of transition, or if you just don't know what looks good anymore *(I'll give you a hint, if you're thinking it's those college sweats, it's not)*. This is not a call for perfection or vanity. This is to encourage you that you're worth it. That your work in the home actually means you can give yourself a manicure every so often if that's your thing. If you want to feel like a boss, then you need to start dressing like one. And watch what this small little step does to transform your psyche.

PRACTICAL THINGS YOU CAN DO TODAY:

1. **Take inventory**
   Holy yo-yo body! How many sizes have you gone through since being a mom?! CLEAN THEM OUT! And I'm talking EVEN THE GOAL JEANS THAT YOU HAVEN'T FIT IN SINCE COLLEGE. Let it go sister. You're not doing anyone any favors by holding on to those cords in your closet that let's be honest, went out of style a few decades ago.

2. Choose wisely

Don't want to break the bank while yo-yoing? I get it! Choose stretchy pants that will rise and fall with you. Go to Nordstrom and get fitted for the right size bra for goodness sakes. It's OKAY to invest in clothes that fit your right-now body. I'm not saying to throw the baby out with the bath water, but make a few strategic choices with your wardrobe so that you feel confident when you have an occasion to step out, or get away with your partner or damnit you just want to feel human for the day. Do it, you're worth it!

3. Share with friends

With each pregnancy, I located a few friends that were roughly my same size, and we just began swapping maternity clothes with one another. The same can apply for going up and coming down clothes. I know that you don't want to spend money on a pair of jean shorts that you'll only wear for one summer, but you do need shorts that will get you through. Consider asking a friend to borrow or trade for the short-term. There's no shame in helping each other out with our closets by sharing clothes that most likely we don't even like.

4. Second Hand, Yes Please!

I am NEVER above a second-hand store. Plato's Closet, the Goodwill or local thrift store, or even ThredUp all are really good options for low-budget, high value pieces of clothes that will help get you through your transitional wardrobe. And even if you don't end up "transitioning" back to a size or shape you once were (*because that's a*

HIGH likelihood), then you can feel good in your current state regardless of the number on the tag or what you used to be. You are not who you used to be. You've birthed actual children (*biologically or not)* and aged actual years – we are not 21 anymore, so stop shopping and wishing and wasting your mental energy thinking we're going back there.

Now that we've tackled the surfaces of our self-care, let's talk a bit about soul care. At my core, I do believe 1000% that self-care *is* soul care, but I do also think that there is an important distinction that is worth making.

Days when I was deep in my depression or ridden with anxiety, having my nails done was all I needed to help me get through the day. Like I said, it was the small act of rebellion that fueled my spirit enough to power through – reminded me that I still had one thing together; my nails. But eventually, once the babies started sleeping, schedules started being more regular, and life seemingly began to balance out into our new normal, I was finding that my soul still felt empty and I still felt lost. I was doing all of the things that all of the self-help gurus had told me to do: I was working out, drinking the water, my nails were done, getting a good night's sleep (*as much as it was in my control)*, even doing my best to do my Bible study on the regular and had even joined a formal Bible study group of women each week. I still felt stuck though and I didn't get it.

What I began to understand and see was that self-help, and self-care was GOOD. These are the things that

175

got me through my darkest days. They were the tangible things that I could control when my everyday life felt wildly out of control. The tantrums from littles that came on out of nowhere, the fever-ridden kid that thwarted the day's plans, or the cough from someone in the house that kept you home from yet another social event. I was grateful for the things that I could control in the realm of self-care, truly I was. But what I began to see is that I needed something more. I needed to root my identity and worth in something greater than just self-help. My days were still dark *(or maybe grey was a better descriptor)* and for some reason, I couldn't muster up that positivity that these self-help preachers were telling me I would receive from their prescribed 4-step method. I was striving. Running daily after all the things, but still coming up short and feeling empty. Maybe if I just do one more workout, I'll feel content. Maybe if I get regular blowouts for my hair AND get my nails done, then I'll really feel put together and will finally be able to tackle my everyday life with purpose. Every single time though, it was empty in the deepest parts of my heart and soul. There was still a part of me that longed for something more. It was a craving that I couldn't really name, but was underneath the self-help steps that I was taking. I was doing all the things and it wasn't working.

Self-care helped me get my head above water and I don't want to downplay the importance of that at all. My prescription for my anti-anxiety meds saved me on days when I could not parent, when I couldn't get out of bed or would get out of bed but would spend the day walking around like a zombie and shell of a person. But it wasn't the thing that was going to sustain me, I began to understand that. Not for the long haul at least – all of the striving, all of the methods were me-focused and just didn't feel sustainable *(even financially)*, and frankly didn't feel like that was really how God had created me to live. I knew deep down that I had to tether my purpose, my soul, my heart, to something bigger, something outside of my own efforts because at the end of the day, I knew I had more to give but I also knew that I sucked at achieving it all on my own. My thoughts slowly began to creep back to the season of life when I felt most alive. What did I have then that I don't have now? And how could I get back to feeling that sense of contentment and purpose without abandoning my current circumstances? Was it possible to feel that deep sense of belonging and purpose without getting rid of my kids? That sounds dramatic, but it's truly what I thought! I couldn't figure out a way to bridge the confident, purposeful, driven me from *before* kids with the slob-kebob always drowning in a sea of chores and children of NOW. I knew that getting rid of my kids and abandoning my life wasn't an option *(unless I wanted to be a Dateline episode)*, so what could I do right now that would bring me that peace inside that I so desperately craved. I so desperately WANTED to feel purposeful in being a mom. I wanted to believe for myself all of the encouraging memes I was posting on Instagram. Because I was finding that I could easily believe them for *you*, but deep down, I didn't believe them for *me*. It just wasn't enough. I needed more.

I went to the only place that I knew had tethered me before, and had proven to be helpful and true in my soul time and again – Jesus.

The dudes that followed Jesus around in his day were called disciples – which is just a fancy word for special friend. So, he had a gaggle of friends who hung with him for the three years that he was formally teaching throughout Jerusalem, and they were always amazed, but always had a spirit of curiosity. Similar to me, they wanted to know the secret to their best life. One day, when he was hanging with his friends and a small crowd of other people *(most likely experts in the Jewish/Hebrew law at the time)*, one of those experts stood up and asked him straight up: what's the secret to life? Jesus coolly answered, "Love the Lord your God with all your heart, with all your soul, with all your strength, and with all your mind; and love your neighbor as yourself." He said if you do this, then you will truly live.[7] This clicked for me. Love God and love my people. The caveat that I hadn't put together was to love with all of my heart, mind, strength, and SOUL. I didn't need more self-care, I needed soul-care. The promise is that when I do that, then I will truly live; I will fully realize that sense of purpose that I so desperately wanted. Soul care was the missing piece to my cravings and longings for purpose. I had spent a lot of time investing in my mind *(parenting books!)*, body *(okay, this is better described as fit-ISH)*, heart *(my heart burst open when I*

[7] Luke 10:25-28 paraphrased

became a mom 1000%), but I hadn't taken the time to nourish my soul. Frankly, I didn't even really know what that meant. And because I had been successful in life and my career prior to being a mom, that I don't think I ever really needed to learn how to engage my soul. It was pretty easy for me to find success in my pre-kids life, that the need to uncover and mine out what was even really deep in my soul just hadn't even been something in my vernacular or toolbelt.

So the soul care path began. And honestly, my entry in was all a little woo-woo for me. I was raised in the Catholic church, and so the rituals of Catholicism were ingrained into my DNA from when I was a young girl. I went to CCD (it's like Catholic kids church), I played with baby Jesus and Mary on the felt cloth board, I was baptized, sat through the most boring-to-me church services, twiddled my thumbs in giant itchy tulle-filled dresses I was forced to wear as my regular Sunday best, and spent my Wednesday nights as a teenager having holy water fights in the sanctuary because that felt like a better use of my time than listening to anything some old person had to teach me about the Bible. The Catholic church was my parents, it was never mine, and so when I began the soul work, I honestly had a little bit of PTSD. My soul didn't want rules and stiff rituals that felt empty to me, I wanted the opposite of that – I wanted what Jesus calls living water. And as I began to peel back layer after layer of childhood PTSD from growing up in a church that I never adopted as my own, I began to see the beauty of the rituals. I started simple and small, little

179

things like breath work. I sought out teachers like Brené Brown, and she taught me box prayers – in for four, out for four. Beth Moore helped me identify destructive familial patterns that had existed for generations that were pure instinct for me, but were not who I wanted to be and not what I wanted to pass along. Jen Hatmaker began to lead the way into a faith where I could be a woman of faith, while still including all of my family and friends that maybe experienced Jesus differently. Sarah Bessey showed me that the feminine and justice parts of my desire, the driver and achiever in me that always wanted to push for more, was actually a beautiful tender part of my existence, not something to be stuffed or squashed. I binged everything Enneagram. And the more that I began to see myself in these beautiful workers, the more my soul began to breathe. It was almost as if I had been striving all this time, searching and searching and searching for purpose coming up empty time and again, until I began the soul work where little by little, I began to release that breath. I was becoming more integrated – mind, body, and soul. Engaging, discovering, and honoring my soul was the final missing piece. For the first time, I felt true freedom in my own skin since becoming a mom. Turns out the soul work was the self-care I needed all along.

CHAPTER 18

The Grass is Greener Where You Water It

Today I'm having one of those days where I just woke up on the wrong side of the bed. I got a full night's sleep, the sun is out, and yet still everything everyone is doing, is DRIVING ME CRAZY! Like the human people that I live with are all of a sudden trying to achieve the Guinness Book of World Record for LOUDEST BREATHER! I mean really people?! I'm all for goals, but loudest breather should not be on the list. For no apparent reason, I am just super irritable. After the typical preschool drop off, I head to the gym by myself thinking that a good walk/run on the treadmill would do the trick – burn off some steam and get a restart on my day. No, as soon as I start to run, my shoe comes untied. Stop, tie the shoe. Headphones back on, keep running. Then, my phone starts blowing up. One thousand people are texting *(damn group texts!)* and interrupting the video that I am trying to focus on and watch during my workout. Argh. I finally silence the world from texting me, try and clear my headspace and suddenly I have to pee! Ugh, I quit. Done. This was a waste of time.

Every so often *(okay, maybe more like at least once a month ifyouknowwhatimsayin)*, I wake up in these funks. I can feel them deep in me from the moment my kids start talking. My immediate gut reaction is to retreat or escape. I want to yell "JUST GO AWAY", but oftentimes this doesn't go over well with my little people. It also may not be the healthiest option, so I just *quietly* retreat and begin to grow bitter. I'm short. I'm snappy. And I'm extremely irritable. Over DUMB things.

Even though my gut instinct is to retreat *(which oftentimes looks like a mindless scroll through Instagram)*, I have found that this merely perpetuates the problem. My instincts don't actually lead me to health or fulfillment. I need to do something to pull myself out of the funk, and usually pretty fast, otherwise the damage from my irritable day will be vast. This comes by way of true discipline. Mind over matter. Trusting that right feelings will follow right actions.

For me, I need the focus off of me and my woes. First, I turn on some music. I love music. I've got playlists for all sorts of occasions. One titled "Get Up" which is my get your butt in gear playlist. One titled "Quiet Time" which is my zen playlist. And one titled "New Stuff" which usually is some combo of Taylor Swift, Justin Bieber, Macklemore and Hillsong. I really connect with melodies and lyrics *(I said that like I know what I'm talking about huh?)*, but really nothing has the ability to change my mood more than music.

After I've got the music going, I can still feel a bit of the funk near the surface. The attention needs off of me, and I need to do something for someone else in the form oftentimes of a random act of kindness. We call them RAOK's in our house. This looks different every time I realize that it's time to pull myself out. Sometimes, it looks like intentionally driving to Starbucks, heading through the drive-thru line and paying for the person behind me. The immediate joy and excitement that you see on the barista's face is priceless, and I promise you, it will change your mood and heart in that moment as well. Sometimes it looks like picking up trash from the ground as I take a walk in the neighborhood. I always tell my kids that character is choosing to do the right thing even when you think no one is looking. So, my Trash Walks I feel like are a real check in my character more than anything. Other times it looks like simply picking up a thing of flowers for a friend or neighbor, or even just sitting in my car in silence while I intentionally send a couple texts to friends to say the positive things I see in them, that we oftentimes don't say in everyday life.

So often we get in these funks and we think that the best solution in order to "fix" our problems is to retreat and work on ourselves. Our instincts and culture often encourage us to pull away from our commitments, resign from that volunteering job you have, quit serving at church, or take a break from hosting monthly book club. Each of these things has a season and a deadline most definitely, but I think that *instead* of pulling back and focusing attention on our own problems and woes, that through *discipline* we actually need to lean in farther to the areas of our life that help us focus on others, or at least require us to be *around* others. This feels and seems SO counter-intuitive, I know this. And focusing on others cannot come at the cost of neglecting your soul-care, or honoring the things that help you breathe, but the project of "you" cannot become the focus of your life. And oftentimes, the change that you are seeking will actually come to you from the inside out when you focus on others.

Perspective is everything. Especially if you are simply just having a bad day, or a bad week, or a bad month. Don't pull away from your community. Lean in. Press in to those relationships and confide in them that you're struggling. Ask them to help you along the way in holding you accountable to showing up. So often, pushing through and persevering will result in right feelings following right actions.

Intentionality, and good intentions are two different things. The grass is not actually greener on the other side, it is simply greener where you water it. You have the power to choose your mood and choose how you engage with it. Here is a short list of some of the simple ways in which I have discovered help pull me out of the funk:

- Head through your nearest coffee or smoothie drive-thru for yourself, and tip 100%

- Pay for someone's groceries at the store

- Swing by Costco and grab a rotisserie chicken and a bagged salad to bring to a friend who is currently struggling – I am of the camp that most problems can be solved with these two things (throw in chips & queso and wine for good measure too)

- Write a note to a friend you're grateful for and drop it in the mail OLD SCHOOL style

- Turn up the music in your car and just dance

- Make a donation to an organization doing something in the world that you care about. Sit and scroll their website to see the good they are bringing to others

- Text that mom friend of yours with teeny tinies – just ask, how are you?

The roller coaster of emotions that my kids will bring into my day is not a ride I am willing to get on anymore. I have to make this choice consciously. Their crazy will not be my crazy today. Or when the last minute, time to get out the door for school scramble is happening, I will calmly say, "Your lack of planning is not my emergency." I am not getting on your crazy train today. In my experience, the funk isn't avoidable. There are just too many variables when it comes to raising kids. The funk will come, some seasons more easily and often than others. There is no recipe for no funk (*that sounds like a disco dance song of our parents' generation...I digress*). But you have a way out, and you have a choice. Water the grass in the areas of gratitude, serving other's, and investing in your own soul care. These will be the tools in your toolbelt that help you weather the storms and the crazy train as it drives by every day. The goal is not perfection, it's just progress. So start small, and watch the seed grow.

On my worst days as a mom, the absolute best sounding thing ever is running away. I have a couple of go-to's – and they usually come in the form of online house hunting or scrolling for cheap tickets to literally anywhere. I open that Redfin app and look at houses for sale in San Diego or Arizona, and then spend a few minutes bee-bopping on over to my Southwest app searching for the cheapest flights for sale to anywhere my dollars will take me, because surely Oakland for $70 will be better than listening to the screaming banshees in my house one more minute. Something inside me just wants to escape. I feel trapped and held hostage in my own home.

One of these particular bad days, I needed out and I needed out bad. You know the ones; the wheels are falling off and it's only 10am. I shot the BFF a text and said, "We need a trip STAT." Like any good BFF, without question, the three little dots appeared on the screen and the words "I'm in" appeared within minutes. This is one of the things that I don't take for granted with my BFF, when she says something, she makes it happen. She's a doer through and through. I quickly hopped on one of my go-to travel apps (*appropriately categorized as "ESCAPE" on my phone*) and within minutes, we had booked a trip to Arizona (*thank the sweet Jesus my parents live there*). Hi ho, hi ho, it's off to mom and dad's I go. I needed adventure. I needed away. Anywhere but at my house.

Isn't it funny how the one place that is supposed to bring us solace and peace, can oftentimes be the one place that we despise and want to escape from? My beautifully shiplapped white walls can oftentimes feel more like a jail cell or detention center, than a scene out of Fixer Upper. I act the part of warden more than mommy-dearest and the inmates are starting to revolt.

In no time, we were on a plane on our way to Arizona. I had nearly caused us to miss our flight by completely oversleeping through my alarm, and when by the time we were supposed to be at the airport, I was just flying out of bed (*which BTW was the middle of the night*) causing such a ruckus in my bedroom, that I woke my poor husband, my bag collapsed open because I didn't zip it efficiently, and I ended up just shoveling all of the contents back in my bag. I didn't care, I had to get to the airport because if we missed this flight, I might just lose my mind. We had our breast pumps in our backpacks (yep, both of us were definitely still nursing full time) and our magazines in hand, nothing would stop us.

When we landed, first thing was first, get to an outlet ASAP before our boobs exploded everywhere. Because of my late awakening, I didn't have time to pump before leaving for the airport, so by this time, I had missed 2.5 feedings from the night and I thought I was going to die. We grabbed our luggage and upon arriving at our destination, flung our bags down and plopped ourselves promptly in front of the nearest outlet to milk ourselves like good mama dairy cows.

Aww...sweet relief.

We labeled our milk stash, and decided that now we could properly begin our sunshine mama getaway. I opened my suitcase that was an absolute mess due to my impromptu pack job post clothes explosion, only to realize that it seemed much fuller than I remembered when I set my bag out the night before. I started sorting through my clothes for my swimsuit (yay for post-partum bikini!) and realized that my bag was in fact much fuller than I had anticipated. Spring time in Arizona typically runs about 85-100 degrees, teetering between hot and extra hot. Most of what I had packed was obviously clothes appropriate for that weather. Sundresses, flowy tank tops, flowy skirts, a couple of wedges to give the illusion of elongated legs, and some more flowy tops because well, post-partum. My suitcase however was filled to the brim with giant stacks of winter sweaters and turtlenecks that I had also brought along. It seemed as though in my middle of the night alarm clock snafu, the contents in which had spilled, had also spilled over into the big pile of donation clothes that I had set aside for the Goodwill. In my hurried and delirious state, I just threw it all in, not remembering or realizing that my whole stack of winter donations was sitting there as well. So instead of packing lightly for this adventure to the sun and pool, I was better prepared for a ski trip to the Alps than a girl's getaway to the desert. God bless it. I packed my entire stack of donation clothes.

I still giggle thinking about that moment to this day. Sitting there going through my suitcase looking for my swimsuit, only to find all of my yo-yo clothes from pregnancy and post-winter pregnancy. Such an idiot.

Running away can be like this though. We want out so badly that it doesn't matter what we bring, prepared or unprepared, anything will be better than where we're at. Except instead of actually running away, and we show up to realize that all of our baggage is actually still with us. Where I run, there I still am. Reality check back into our real lives that I can't escape the donation pile from back home. It is sort of like a boomerang. In the thick of momming all day every day, I just want someone to chuck me as far as the arm can throw. I just want to escape. Anywhere, anytime, winter, spring, summer or fall – it all sounds great. I always think that I'll enjoy the view from way far away for a good chunk of time. Until I don't. About three to four days is my max (*although I'm willing to push it to 7-10 if anyone wants to watch my kids for that long).* Then I'm ready to come back home. I need the clarity oftentimes that I get from running away, to see that I'm actually a mess whether at home or in Arizona, and running away won't actually solve my problems (*although tequila poolside sure does the trick for a few hours).*

Maria Goff in her book *Love Lives Here* speaks to this concept of adventure when she says, "When we finally get to the edges of our lives, we understand what is at the center of them." When we finally get away, when we get the opportunity to escape, it is then that we can see through the fog and understand that home is actually where we want to be. Cuddling a snuggly baby is so much better than being milked by a machine round the clock. The little people need you, and frankly, you need them. We were made like this. To need each other.

I've spent a lot of days running away, or longing to run away. Most of those reasons had everything to do with the children and most of the reasons for my return each time were the children. Your problems are still there, even when running. You escape to the valley of the sun, only to find that you've packed your winter wardrobe even though you thought you had dealt with it and shed that skin. The same things that seemingly drive us away, are also there to welcome and call us back home. There is no escaping motherhood. There is no running away. The only way through it, is through it. Seek adventure and get to the end of yourself. It is so so so healthy to do this. But after you've had your moment, after you've realized that your life isn't actually better away from them, but rather with them, come back home. Boomerang back to the place that launched you. Because that is where the good stuff is. That is where you are meant to be, snuggling them, loving on them, and running that Cruise ship.

CHAPTER 19

Live With Intention

"This was a giant waste of my time." –said no mom ever binging The Bachelor

One thing that I have known for sure since the very beginning of our marriage, was that we both were passionate about this idea of legacy. Traditionally, most people think of financial legacy when we hear that word, but for us it became clear early on that legacy for us was a much richer value that went way deeper than just financial provision for generations. This type of legacy is a value that we wanted at the core of our family, outside of just money. It first was presented to us by witnessing the parents of a dear college friends' story of legacy. His parents had chosen to uproot their family, and build a community where community previously didn't exist. Their story of intentionally picking up their lives and moving to do something together with their friends, struck a chord deep within me. I couldn't really articulate *why* I was so drawn to their story; all I knew was that I wanted that in my life too. We walked into their life 20+ years into their intentional community building phase and it was so deep and rich, that I knew a life with intentionality focused on community was an absolute must in our core family values. We wanted legacy in our life.

Over the years, I have come to identify that God has made me a builder. Not a hang out at Home Depot with my hammer and tools kind of builder. No, no, that is much too complicated for my skillset. More like a people builder. Or better yet, a community builder.

This has looked different in different seasons, but oftentimes, I have found myself in a role or place to build an infrastructure, a system, a team, a legacy, and then we move on. It was this way in my career pre-kids, and post-kids these have been volunteer positions as well. I have always been able to see a need, pitch a vision, and put it into action. This is a gift and I recognize that. My frustration would come though, when we'd move on *(ie having another baby and having to shift my focus on growing a child or something of the like)* and I don't get to enjoy the fruits of this "thing" (whatever that is) that "I" have built. Yet, as we continued to come back to this idea of legacy, we realized that the building of it had to start with intentionality. These things that we adored, desired, and oftentimes *envied* in the lives of others *(particularly surrounding really rich friendships and long-lasting community)* all came as a part of some very intentional choices by someone along the way. Legacy is not an overnight thing, despite what our American culture tells us. We want the quick fix, the immediate gratification of a solid friendship or influential presence in our neighborhood, and it actually takes grit and time to build. We are quick to throw in the towel on friendships, or lifestyles, because you've been trying for six months and don't have "it". Nope, I call BS.

As I began to work my way out of the fog of the little years, I began to realize that I had all of the tools at my fingertips to possess the life that I had always wanted. I did some personal growth work, and began to understand and believe some key themes about who God had made me to be.[8] God has equipped me as a builder, so I began to give myself permission to lean in to that and apply it where I was at. That looked like being intentional about how and where we start building, in order to get where I wanted to go.

---

[8] If you are at this crossroads and trying to navigate where you are supposed to go. Start with understanding who and how God has wired you. There are so many great resources out there, but I particularly chose to do *Breaking Free* by Beth Moore to understand my family of origin and where I came from, Jennie Allen's *Restless* to see patterns God had already woven in my life in regards to pain and giftings, and then learning about my Enneagram type. Those three things should give you some insights and hopefully will help illuminate next steps for you to start making some headway in your life.

Each one of us possesses this same opportunity. We all have influence. Every single one of us. Insecurity and shame may be telling you to shrink back or not believe in the fact that you, in the exact phase and stage of life you're in right now, have influence. You need to start by acknowledging that. And then once you acknowledge it, you need to be intentional about how you're going to use it. We had to sit down and decide together what we wanted our life to look like. We needed to decide that we wanted a great marriage, and then we could fill in the pieces on how we were going to be intentional about building that. We decided that we wanted a rich community of neighbors and friends for us and our kids. And then we had to start building that. For lack of a better term, we created a vision for our life and worked backwards. This was crafted overtime through intentional conversations – and wasn't done formally at like a weekend retreat (*although that would be cool and legit*). Ours was more organically developed over time through intentional conversation. Although I do have a friend who hired a personal development coach to sit down with their family and walk them through an actual mission and vision statement formally with their family but it is not required for you to go to that extreme.

I think in the age of social media, we oftentimes fall into the trap that these intangible things that we all would ultimately say we want for our life (legacy, healthy kids, rich friendships, fun community, etc.) just *happen* for other people, or they live in the "right" neighborhood and your neighborhood sucks and it's just not like that. That is just garbage. You have to decide to be the builder. And be intentional. And guess what, IT'S HARD! It is going to take time! And ultimately requires serious planning and vulnerability.

My Saturday nights aren't just filled up with super fun hang outs and gatherings with our friends because people just wandered up to our door. We had to put ourselves out there and risk exposure in the midst of our daily messes, in order to find the richness and zest toward life that we craved. We had to recognize that building these things was going to come at a cost. It has required sacrifice, and oftentimes, that looks very practical in our finances.

I am a full time mom that has a babysitter part time to help us during the week. When I share this fact with other moms, both full time working outside and inside of the home, I am often met with a lot of judgement. *Umm what do you mean you have a babysitter when you stay at home?* I understand their judgement and I recognize that it is very much a privilege to have help. For us, the priority was getting me help with childcare and that could free me up to clean our house or do the other tasks of managing a household that would help me keep my sanity. I'd rather hire childcare help and put my headphones on to listen to podcasts while I spend 2-3 hours cleaning my toilets and scrubbing my floors. That's just me though. I know plenty of others that would sell their left kidney before they cancelled their house cleaner, in order to just spend five more minutes playing with their kids. Regardless, there is help in both scenarios. The general census around help and moms though is that it's not okay.[9] We have goals as a family, and for us, we realized early on, that one of the ways that we were going to be able to achieve these goals was going to be getting me help. And it was going to cost us something. So what were we going to have to do, or let go of, in order to get us there?

There is absolutely no way that we could do our life without our part-time babysitter. Now I fully realize that we are very fortunate enough to afford this type of opportunity and I'm speaking from a place of privilege, but my point is not to brag or sound Real Housewives-esque, but more to speak to the fact that we have had to arrange our finances – even in the early years when we had NO MONEY, to reflect our goals and priorities. One of those was my mental health *(thank you babysitter)*, one of those was our marriage (*babysitter hours has to include regular date night*), and one of those was the ability to consistently connect with our friends on a deeper level which requires intentional time spent with them *without* the children. When the children aren't there to distract, conversations can actually *go there*, and that's when you start to see the depth of legacy emerging. If you want the intangibles of life, just know

---

[9] Many people have the local help of their families for childcare. We did not. Judgement merely seems to come when you *pay* for outside, not when you just *have* it. But what happens when you don't have a choice but to pay? Yes, that's where we were at.

that they are going to come at a cost. The saying goes, "the best things in life are free" and I call BS on that. It's rather misleading. Sure, the *fruit* of the things in life might be free, but someone had to plant that tree, water it, pluck it, care for it, prune it, etc. in order for you to walk by and enjoy the fruit. Our legacy will come through the investments that we make into our everyday lives. Don't discount what you are already doing. Also, don't miss what you aren't doing. Set a vision for your life and begin working toward it. Only you will be able to articulate your family's values and priorities which will ultimately lead to your family's legacy. We get one life, the day to day matters and counts, and there is so much purpose in it.

CHAPTER 20

Heart Work is Hard Work (Let's Talk About Sex Baby)

In life, it is not the things we achieve, but the person we become. Decisions will feel less heavy if we truly believe that.

–Emily P. Freeman

Nothing has been more of a grind, or more daily, in my journey of motherhood than our marriage. When we got married at 22 (*babies!*), we had NO IDEA what was in store for us. If I'm being honest, I actually thought our marriage was going to be easy and blessed. And I naively thought this primarily because of one thing: morality.

Our story is a bit of an outlier and something that isn't normal. Both Blake and I chose early on in our young adult lives (*separately obviously*) to save sex for marriage. I know, gasp! This is virtually unheard of these days, and if I'm being honest, was something that I actually felt shame and insecurity about in the beginning years. We had no "street cred" amongst our friends, and received judgement for it (*still do oftentimes when it comes up in conversation with new-ish friends*). We wanted to save that gift for our future spouse because of our personal faith convictions. This was something that I prayed over regularly and held in very high regard internally.[10] I held this card up high with pride all throughout high school and college, and hope with every ounce of being in my heart that my little girl grows up to feel the same way about her sexuality someday. Anyway, because we both chose to save ourselves for marriage, I thought since we had done it "right", that our reward would be an easy marriage. Newsflash, that was not the case! In our dating life, it required so much intentional work to NOT go past our invisible "line" physically (*that's the morality piece*), that I thought for sure as long

---

[10] Side note: it actually makes me REALLY sad that being a virgin is such a shame thing these days and gets made fun of all the time. If I ever hear about someone shaming my son or daughter for NOT having sex, I will cut you. Mama bears beware. □

as we could make it (*technically of course*) to the finish line of our wedding night, it would be smooth sailing from there on out. A lifetime of marital bliss, especially in the bedroom, for waiting to have sex until we were married. This would be the payoff for years of waiting. Ha! Again, we were babies when we said 'I do'. We had no clue.

Fast forward, as we are now about to celebrate our 12th year of marriage, and our sex life has begun to age like a fine wine. We're finally getting better and better. Although we've moved past the initial awkward and hard days of bedroom woes in our marriage, there definitely was a season of really hard things that we had to push and work through in our sex life. The reality that I have learned is that anything good comes from hard, consistent, and intentional work. These things that we are hoping to achieve – solid marriage, grateful kids, mental health – all of them come at a high cost of work. Heart work is hard work. And unfortunately there just isn't a shortcut. Trust me, I've tried. There also is no reward for simply living a life of morality for the sake of morality. We teach our children right and wrong, and if we're honest, most of us all just instinctively recognize the difference between right and wrong. But living a moral life does not bring the depths of joy, purpose or peace that offer contentment to our souls as we lay our heads down on the pillow each night.

Case in point: adding a third kid to our family. We had two rowdy boys and I had that ache in my heart that our family wasn't yet complete. Blake and I went round and round on this decision for months. He was less excited to catapult our parenting into "zone defense" and I couldn't argue with him. All of the reasons on paper, I totally agreed with. The world is definitely meant for two kids. Cars are meant for two kids. Rides at theme parks work perfectly for families of four. But that just wasn't in my heart. It didn't make logical sense; it was just what I felt. I knew it would be *the hardest* thing we took on. I had already battled postpartum depression with baby #2, still didn't have the built-in safety net of family in the area, yet my heart still longed for that third baby. In addition to that, I had really high-risk pregnancies and we knew that trying for another munchkin wouldn't be an easy path. This wasn't going to be easy for our marriage.

I'm sure you've heard the statistics by now that one in every two marriages ends in divorce. Having walked this path with several friends, we knew that some serious boundaries were going to need to be put in place in order for us to beat those statistics. Especially in parenting. For us, that has meant implementing weekly date night. We have had to figure out a way to connect, even in the little years, despite the chaos and neediness going on around us, in order to regularly remember that we like each other and are on the same team. Now, mind you, in the early itty-bitty years of our marriage and parenting days when we barely had a dime to our name, it meant that we had to get creative with how we were going to achieve this. But regardless of our socioeconomic status, it was a value that we knew we wanted because we ultimately wanted to choose each other at the end of the day, and we knew (*from watching other marriages around us dissolve*) that in order to make it out of this parenting journey with our marriage intact, that it was going to take a million little things along the way to get us there. We couldn't wait until the golden parachute of money bags fell into our lap to begin fighting for, and working toward, a good marriage.

So, we started with what was free. Books on marriage, podcasts (*those weren't really a thing when we first had kids*), walks with babies and kids in strollers – all small ways that we began to build in as regular rhythms to connect. Blake was working long hours when we had babies and was commuting at least two hours a day, so there were plenty of days when he didn't even get home until after at least one or two of the babies were in bed which meant no walks. Which meant we had to flex. Flexibility in the day to day has been SO key and is a constant learning process for us because what flexibility butts up against is expectations, and sometimes unmet expectations, and unmet expectations tend to cause tension and/or resentment. If I was momming at home by myself all day long (*say, taking care of sick littles for the billionth time in the winter months*) and I was looking forward to that adult connection time as soon as he got home, but then there was traffic, and the baby had to go down early, and all of a sudden the one thing that I was looking forward to all day was pulled out from underneath me. And usually due to no fault of either of us – it was just life with littles! In those scenarios, I could choose to allow the bitterness and resentment build, and storm off to pout into the bedroom for the rest of the evening (*which I have done COUNTLESS times mind you*), or I could flex.

And flexing goes both ways. Let's take a deep breath for a minute because we're going to go there. *breathes in, breathes out* Sex. In the little years of caring for babies who need you physically and emotionally all day long, the desire for sex from one partner (*bet you can't guess which this applied to in our relationship!*) can oftentimes be about 4,000 items *down* on the list of wants and needs. We knew though that regular sex was a hallmark for people around us who had thriving marriages – even in the little years! As sad and heartbreaking as it was, the little years seemed to be the *most* frequent time friends around us began experiencing major hurts in their marriages. Infidelity and hidden porn addictions *during* the baby years became a regular thing that would come out in our social circles. And I think oftentimes it is easy to blame the men or have empathy for the women, but the reality is that sex has to occur inside the relationship on a regular basis from *both* parties in order to make a marriage work. Recognizing that you're both working super hard, and it's emotionally and physically exhausting for BOTH of you, not just one. I'll never forget when I walked in on Blake watching porn one night. I was probably six months pregnant with Brecken, I had been throwing up and felt like garbage for *months* and we definitely were not having regular sex. Porn was not an outlet that we had agreed to in our marriage and I felt extremely betrayed. *How could you? Am I not good enough? I'm over here growing a BABY and you're so concerned about your sexual needs that you can't even wait?!* It was bad and extremely hurtful. I was devastated and immediately retreated emotionally. Thankfully, we had friends around us who had walked this path before. We slowly mended the hurt, began to build trust again (*with seriously clarified new boundaries we put in place for accountability)*, and both of us – for the first time – understood what our role was to move forward. I knew regular sex was on me just as much as it was on him, and that parenting and kids could not be an excuse for why we weren't having it regularly. In hindsight, I'm so thankful that I found out about the porn at that time, because it allowed us to begin talking openly about sex with one another for the very first time. It opened the door for us to honestly, and vulnerably, share with each other what our needs were. The taboo stigma around sex in a marriage, especially in Christian culture, has to stop. You're married – it's time to start talking about sex! This is going to sound weird I know, but we even gathered some friends from our church (women with women, men with men) and created a safe space to talk about sex. We read excerpts from therapists and marriage experts on what a good sex life entailed. It opened the door for the subject to basically not be taboo, not only in our own marriage, but also in our friendships with those closest with us. Because let's address the elephant in the room, we all were cranking out babies – sex was happening at least once every nine months minimum.

Sex needs to be talked about between you and your partner in order to have a thriving marriage. Yeah, with each pregnancy and each post-partum season, it has been challenging. But we flex with one another and we talk about it. The door is open for one of us to regularly say, "Hey, I'm not getting what I need right now" or "I'm feeling this sort of way with how little we've connected lately". It is safe to communicate these things with one another. Find me a thriving marriage that isn't having regular sex. I just don't think the two go together. A thriving marriage equals a thriving sex life. And frankly, as women, we need to own vulnerable communication with our partners on this too. It has taken me a lot of years to get to this point, but we are modern day women, and the whole "damsel in distress" in the bedroom, isn't cute or "proper" anymore. You are free to talk with your partner about what you want too, or what feels good. We are strong and educated, not women from the *Leave it to Beaver* age anymore. So, let's translate that to the bedroom. Have fun with it! Capitalize on seasons in between growing and pushing out babies when it is good. Blake and I have worked for years to get to the point where we build in one overnight date a month. There's something magical that happens for both of us when we get out of our everyday environment and go somewhere else (*hello hotel sex!*). If I just lost you because you're thinking there's absolutely zero chance you could afford to go to a hotel every month, then you've missed the point. There is no formula for how or when or where. For a good sex life it's going to require you both to be flexible with one another, intentional about your timing, which you can discover through good communication. Talk to your partner and have the hypothetical conversations about how frequently they would like to have it, what's reasonable, what feels good, what definitely is a major turn off, etc. These are free things and don't have to cost a million dollars. You can't buy your way to a solid marriage (*although counseling does go a long way*), but you can communicate and flex with each other toward one. Heart work in your marriage is going to be hard work. It will not be bliss all the time especially in the chaos of pregnancies, babies, and toddlers. But good can be achieved with some elbow grease, grit, commitment, and determination to walk out of the fire on the other side still holding hands. We need more good marriages in our world, and I know that's what you want for yourself in the long run too. Just know that it means starting right now, right in the middle of the mess of your everyday world. Heart work is hard work.

CHAPTER 21
No Bailouts

Nothing feels more exhausting or fruitless at times, then measuring if you are actually getting through to the hearts of your little people. How many times do I gently remind them to say thank you, before I just lose my ever-loving mind when on the 100th time they STILL don't say thank you? Like I swear I am talking about, and teaching them gratitude and really trying to not raise little ~~shits~~ terds. Where I realized I was going wrong though was thinking that their lack of response to my correction and teaching, was in direct-relation to my success as a mom. So if my kids were acting like Satan-inhabited gremlins, that obviously must be reflective of the job that I am doing, and ultimately who I am. If my fulltime job is solely to raise and influence these kids and I can't even get that right, what good am I?

It wasn't until I got the courage to jump off their crazy train and separate my worth and identity from their choices, that I began to find a bit of freedom. No number of reminders, systems, yelling matches, timeouts, or chores are going to penetrate their hearts no matter how hard I try. They have to choose to allow to be transformed from the inside out the same way that I have had to, and that is on them. Yes, it is my job to guide and direct and help strategize and introduce, but I will no longer be riding their crazy train, because it's exhausting and if I put too much of me into their choices, then that train quickly derails.

How this practically looks in my household is like this. Recently, all of the hype was being touted for the upcoming book fair at school. The teachers and the blessed PTA do a fantastic job of sending home catalogs pimping various books for the kids to purchase, advertisements and reminders online and in the classrooms. Needless to say, my kids were stoked. Their very own mall was coming to their school. Each class has allotted times where they get to "shop". Now obviously there are *way* worse things for my kids to be spending their money on than books, but also, these books are available FOR FREE in the local library. I digress. Anyway, of course my children buy in to all of the marketing and hype and want to participate in the Book Fair. They whole-heartedly believe that this will be their last chance at these magnificent books for sale at school. Bless them. So I finally gave in and allow said children to spend their money on these books. Fine, that's how you want to spend it, go ahead.

Well, the special shopping day rolls around and both kids have been waiting with eager anticipation to purchase their chosen items from the book fair. The only thing standing between them and their loot, is remembering to bring their money. One child is super responsible and in no way, no how was he going to forget his money. Grabs it, I double check he hasn't carelessly thrown in a Benjamin or something, and he's on his merry way. Low and behold, the *other child* has a slightly harder time remembering things, even things that are important to him. The day of the book fair arrives, and the excitement and anticipation are palpable. The only thing we can seem to talk about at breakfast is all the things that can be bought at the book fair (*I mean at one point, I was even feeling like gosh, I better head over to shop those carts of books because who knows what sort of deals I can find on glitter pencil pouches and the Big Nates series!*) The forgetful child of mine "forgets" to set aside time to gather his money and jumps OFF the bus as he is packing up to head off for the day, and yells to me from down the street, "Mom, run home and grab my money on my nightstand for the book fair." I stand there for a minute not sure if I should be mad, pissed or proud of his assertive and demanding words clearly expressed in a time of distress for him. My immediate response is, "Oh I'm sorry – do I work for you?" In hindsight, maybe I could have responded with a bit more tenderness and empathy in my voice rather than just being flippant, but I'll do better next time. ▯ #okayestmomever After a minute of contemplation of how to responsibly respond, I get my bearings and more

213

effectively communicate a more mature response. "Nope, sorry. Love you buddy." No sir, I ain't doing it, and back on the bus he goes.

Well this kid has some serious negotiating skills because as I'm sipping my now lukewarm coffee enjoying the bliss of a quiet home that only comes when those blessed rug rats get on the bus, my email notifications ding. I look down at my inbox to an email from said son's teacher titled "Forgotten Book Money". The email says:

Dear Mrs. Carbonatto, I am letting Brecken write you an email. See below.

HI MOM, I FORGOT MY BOOK MONEY. YOU CAN GRAB MY WALLET WITH $10 IN IT ON MY NIGHTSTAND AND BRING IT TO SCHOOL. THANK YOU. LOVE B

Oh hell no.

Once I was able to process what was happening, and realize he must've hit the caps lock button and wasn't really yelling at me, but was giving a sincere *(albeit rather manipulative)* try for me to bring his book fair money, I took a deep breath and hit reply:

Dear Mrs. [Lovely Teacher], thank you for the email. See below.

Hi B, I unfortunately won't be able to bring you any book fair money today. Your lack of preparation is not my emergency. Let's see if we can figure out a reminder for you tonight when you get home so that hopefully you can remember to bring it tomorrow. I love you bud, Love Mom

I don't care if your only plan for the day was to paint your nails and catch up on This Is Us, you do not owe that kid a day's worth of interruptions because he was lazy and couldn't remember to bring his money. Nope. Not doing it. And the truth of the matter is that I was legit scared when I hit reply and send to his teacher. I was scared of the judgement that might come. The judgement that geez, she's a SAHM, what ELSE is she doing today? Or thinking that my kid might be the *only* one during their allotted shop time who has to sit out and can only window shop at best for the day.

Bummer. Nope, not going to be guilted from other people's perceptions of "good mom" into robbing my kid of a natural consequence, no matter how unpopular that might make him.

Our goals as moms is to raise the best humans possible. And yes, we have grace upon grace in this house, but in the same vein, when I set them up for success and they choose not to take the reins of implementation for themselves, that is just not my problem. I will guide them. I will be there for them. And I will continue to expect progress, not perfection while offering grace. But there are some times in which it is OKAY, and dare I say RIGHT, for you to not have to stop whatever it is that *you're* doing just to rescue and save *their* irresponsibility. The fallout from that is on them. It is 100% their lesson to learn naturally. It

215

could've been a bad day at school. Forgotten homework. Forgotten lunch even. And my answer would have been the same.

Like I said before, heart work is hard work ladies. And is going to require some boundaries for us to not always interrupt our lives to rescue and save them. I believe that my only hope for getting the intangible character traits to soak into their little hearts and take hold of them as they grow and launch into the world as young adults, is if I start to take away their safety net when reasonable. Jen Hatmaker wisely said in her book *For The Love*, "A wise parent prepares the child for the path, not the path for the child." My worth and identity is not tied to them, or their choices, or their lack of choices. I have had to learn to accept this *(sometimes daily)* in order to keep the end goal of raising kind humans in mind. This was so freeing for me once I started to believe it to be true. I hope you feel freedom in that. I want them to experience and adapt to grit and perseverance in the same way that I want those traits too. If I'm always rescuing them, even as young as Kindergarten or 1st grade, then I'm just ultimately adding to the pressure as a mom that I already experience, and I'm setting them up for a reality that just isn't true. It's a lose-lose. When they forget their book fair money, that is their lesson to learn not mine.

My son's teacher ultimately replied with words of encouragement for me stating that for that day, I was in fact her hero. And that she then shared my soft rejection with the rest of the 1ˢᵗ grade staff over lunch, which was received with cheers and high fives I'm told. And you want to know what? Guess who came home and FIRST THING went upstairs and grabbed his wallet to set by his backpack for the next day to bring to school? All on his own. No reminders. Why? Because it was a message he was learning from the inside out. Not from a lecture. Not from a safety net. But from trial and error. The same as we have had to learn in our own adult lives.

Let's not add to our pressure as moms. We *already* do so much, have so many other insecurities and expectations that not only the world puts on us, but that we put on each other. We don't need to be adding to that. And the minute that you sign up to save your child each time they have an opportunity to fail, you are robbing them of the chance to learn the heart work on their own. I've always had to learn the hard way, why would I expect my kids to be any different? Let's take back our lives. Take back our homes. You have permission to let them fail! We can give our kids the jobs, and the lessons, that are rightfully theirs to learn. Each situation and kid will be different. Sometimes our responses can be ones that they do not deserve, that are just laden with grace. And that's great – there is 1000% a time and place for this. We are tender and I want them to know that I am always, always in their court. But I will not operate out of fear, pressure or expectation that *my* job and purpose is to serve and work for them. No ma'am. I love them too much to let them think they are the center of my universe. Because someday, I want them out there in the world influencing and changing hearts of the next generation after me. And that's not going to happen if mama taught them that they make the world go round.

CHAPTER 22

People Matter, Invite Them Over

We love to host. In each of the homes and spaces that we have inhabited and owned, this has been a core value of ours. Hosting formally is not for everyone. But I do believe that inviting people into your spaces on a regular and consistent basis *is* for everyone. And is actually something that we should be doing.

I have a sign that hangs in our dining room that says "Family Gathers Here". We adapted the mantra that "friends are family" many moons ago. It was right about when we had our first-born son that both of our extended families decided to trade in the constant Seattle rain for perma-sunny Arizona life. This was super confusing to us at first – we had just moved back from our newlywed adventure in Los Angeles, in order to settle down and be closer to our families. Everyone had been on our case for months about babies and grandchildren and rushing into that next phase of life to fulfill some unmet role in their life. Yet, when we made it happen, they bounced. We found ourselves knee-deep with little babies, with no built-in support system. Our extended family was not a part of our everyday life in the way that we had envisioned (*or seen on Full House*).

We instantly realized, friends would be considered family as well. Our friends are not just a part of our life, they ARE our life. Showing up for, and with them, is just as important to us as our own family. These are the ones who choose to walk through each phase of life with us. You're having a baby? I want to throw a party to celebrate. Why? Not because I just LOVE the stress of planning a party so much, but more so because people matter. And celebrating them matters.

At the start of each year, Blake and I sit down and brainstorm some of the themes of gatherings that we want to be a part of that year because we've found that it's easier to make friends when we are fun, and do fun things *(that's a free tip – being fun attracts fun people. Boring things attract boring people – you get to decide which you want to be!)*. Oftentimes, we can't predict when we're going to throw a Gender Reveal party or things of that nature, but there are some fun things that we'd just rather do together with friends, than by ourselves. Some of the ideas we've already done, and/or have on our bucket list to host are:

- Cinco de Mayo party. This also happens to be our anniversary, so what better excuse to bring people together than for tacos, tequila and US! ☺

- Kentucky Derby party. Oh my word, this has been a serious bucket list party idea of mine for YEARS. I want everyone in their Sunday best, big hats are a MUST, mint juleps on tap, and betting. Yes, definitely betting. It will be a fab party someday.

- Cioppino. My husband has deep Italian heritage, so sharing this family recipe of seafood stew, gathered around a long inclusive table of everyone sounds like the best time and reason to gather and celebrate.

- Bring your favorite teriyaki takeout party. You might be thinking this is a stretch, but who doesn't love a good teriyaki takeout. We live in the Greater Seattle area, and teriyaki is a *thing* here. We need to know who has THE BEST. Blind taste tests – these are a thing and a great way to bond with your neighbors (*and requires no cooking or house prep*).

Life is just so much better in groups.

I get it, having a zillion people over with a zillion kids sounds like a nightmare for some, including me every other day. And when they are all super little, and you're spending most of your time chasing after the little's to keep them from trying to kill themselves, then yes, it is a bit of a nightmare, I would agree. I suggest doing more NO KID hangouts in this season. Or, we've been known to do dinner "parties" in shifts – feed the kids first, fill their little bellies and promptly plop their little butts in front of a screen for group movie night. Then the adults can sit and enjoy a beverage, meal, and the joys of uninterrupted conversation without having to hire a babysitter. But as the kids grow, it has become easier to just embrace the chaos. This is a choice of course. Would I prefer a quiet atmosphere where we can have great uninterrupted conversation? Of course. But we also chose to have kids, and when I keep our family values in mind of showing them that community is how we are meant to be living, then that means that I have to embrace the chaos of a quadrillion kids from time to time.

Inviting people in is messy and will cost you something. There is no magic formula on how to have people over, or in, or celebrating, without it being a bit chaotic or costing you something. This is just the reality. Find your people, and if you feel like you don't have them, then start with one couple. One family. And invite them over. If they are weird, don't invite them again. ☺ But keep trying. Finding friends, and making friends in adulthood is like dating. You might not find your one true love on the first date. But stick with it. Your people are out there. Keep doing the things that you already love doing, and keep your eyes open for the others that are there doing it too. And then ask them on a date – just kidding, but it does feel a bit like awkward interviewing/dating when you make new friends. This is normal, stay the course. Raising littles is so hard, so lonely, and so monotonous –

you *need* your people. And when you find them, don't let them go. Celebrate, embrace, and gather often. Because that is where the good stuff happens. Your soul will feel full even when your house is a mess and your fridge is empty. It doesn't make sense, but I promise it to be true.

CHAPTER 23

Becoming a Dreamer...Again

Have you ever had a dream in your heart? Maybe you're standing in the shower with no distractions, or driving in the car kidless (*that actually sounds like a dream in an of itself*), and all of a sudden you catch a vision – you see a glimpse or picture of a life, or part of a life, that you want. And you think, "I could do that!" "I could be that!" Your brain starts racing and the ideas are flowing – it is clear as day. This sort of thing happens to me regularly. I think part of it is just because I was designed to be a dreamer, and I think part of it is because somewhere deep inside I feel stuck in my role as a mom at home, and I'm constantly trying to ensure that I'm living a full life in all capacities.

These dreams though that are born inside of us, they are something that is most likely from a deep place in our heart. You want to run a marathon, yet you've never even run a mile. You have dreams of standing on a stage and speaking to teach hundreds, but you won't even volunteer to pray out loud at dinner. And let's say you do get the courage to even just speak these things out loud to people you trust – that is SCARY! I can't tell you how many times I have brought a dream in hand to a trusted friend, advisor, sister, or even my husband, pitched it a bit to only have it met with anything but wild excitement and celebration. I think what people who haven't walked through the wilderness of losing themselves to motherhood or any sort of identity crisis of uncertainty in their everyday, they don't understand the giant gap that you have had to walk even just to get back to a spot where you CAN dream, let alone finding the courage to articulate it out loud. So more times than not, I share my dream or vision with someone (*even trusted someones*), it's met with less than stellar excitement (*because again, when you're telling someone you want to run a marathon but haven't even run a mile they're looking at you like wow...you've got a WAYS to go lady*). But here's the thing: in order to take action on your dream, it CANNOT be dependent on the approval of others. If something has been born in your heart, oftentimes you're the first one in on the secret! You got the playbook first! And yes, it would be amazing if someone else ALSO got that playbook simultaneously and now you guys get to run together, but let's assume they didn't (*because they most likely didn't*), then it's up to you to start running those plays. Your people might not fully get it, even the ones who are 100% in your court. They don't see with clarity your vision and dream.

Yet.

Even though you both are at the starting line, you saw the finish line, and all they can see is mile 1 and it looks steep and hard. This is totally understandable!

Your job: run anyway.

Trust me, I know this is easier said than done. I am sitting here typing this out on the heels of pitching a pretty big dream of mine to some dear friends and my partner, and it sort of flopped. The vision was not caught. And I don't think they got it. And even though no one said anything negative, I don't think I realized and prepared myself enough for how vulnerable it was for me to even share. Big dreams and visions often start with just one step. And when you're standing at the edge of decision, determining whether or not to jump or if you should wait for a bridge to be built across, sometimes the answer is jump. Even as I type that, my heart sinks. That is SO SCARY! What if I fail? What if I jump, and no one gets it still? What if it costs me money and time that I don't have right now? This type of fear can, and will, paralyze you. It has me for years! Like I said, I've been dreaming for YEARS. But I get lost in the future-tripping of not understanding how it will all work out. I can't see the steps of how the dots will be connected, and I want to just be at the finish line already. When it's hard, or the path looks totally unknown, I quit. I've done it a thousand times – just ask my husband. And then I'll use the excuse when my people don't fully get it either (*because duh, it wasn't their dream!*) to fulfill my self-doubt and I can point to it and say, "see, that wasn't even meant to be my path." But I'm becoming really tired of allowing my fears to prevent me from just DOING IT. Going scared, and just TRYING. Marie Forleo, in her book, _Everything is Figureoutable_, asks the question, "In ten years, will I regret NOT doing this?"[11] And in this season of life, with this particular dream, reading that question stopped me dead in my tracks. The answer was absolutely 100% YES, I will regret not just jumping NOW.

Motherhood can, will be, and is all consuming. We are raising babies into children into teenagers into actualy real live humans. I'm sure for a lot of us, those kids that are causing us the anxiety and overwhelm and stress were actually a dream at one point. We dreamed of being a mom. Some of us didn't have motherhood on the radar, or it has been a path that has arrived in a much more unexpected manner. Either way, the bill of goods that we are sold is that motherhood is dreamy. So, what happens when it's not? Is it okay to have a dream outside of motherhood? Am I a bad mom for wanting to speak on a stage, or write a book, or start a podcast, or not volunteer in the classroom? I wish I had a formula for you on this, but there isn't one. With 100% certainty I

[11] Marie Forleo, *Everything is Figureouable*, page 155

can tell you that you are not a bad mom at all if you have dreams in your heart that seem at the outset to interrupt your path of motherhood. Reese Witherspoon says it this way, "Ambition is not a dirty word." Maybe staying at home worked for a season, but now it's not. Or vice versa, maybe you have been a kick ass career woman leading the charge for women in the workplace, but now the dream looks more like spending more hours at home. Our dreams will evolve, and they won't look the same from mom to mom, from generation to generation, and from season to season. It is our job as women to honor the dream that is in our heart right now. Hold it up to the filters of your values, see how it matches with your giftings, your passions, and the long game for what you want out of life. Sure, logistically, it might not make any sense for your family life situation right now (*i.e. but who will watch all of these kids?!*). I tell you this with such tenderness and grace and moxie, but the best tool I have to offer is to just figure it out. When I think of how many years I have suppressed, put off, and not done the work to honor the dreams in my own heart – like writing this book – it makes me so sad. Mostly for me. It makes me sad that I've been momming for so long, feeling like these little years of daily life was an everyday uphill battle for me where none of my natural giftings were in play. I've told you I suck in the kitchen and domestically am vastly an underachiever. And the story that I started to tell myself around that was that I ultimately sucked. That I was terrible at my entire role as a mom. Mentally, I began to just throw the baby out with the bath water. I buried my dreams so deep that it felt like motherhood was more a season of life that I had to *endure* rather than live and *enjoy*. When I started to think about that life for my daughter – one where she so clearly was gifted in specific ways, but lived small in fear and doubt, and questioned every bit of her self-worth and identity, it legit makes me cry. I knew I needed to mine for those dreams again, and create the space, no matter how much it didn't make sense, to bring them to light. It meant accepting failure. I needed to get really comfortable with falling flat on my face, while other people were watching. It meant accepting that failing at something wouldn't change any of my inherent value or worth. Just because I might try and fail at something did not make me a failure. Nope, that value and worth to dream and be a dreamer, was something no role or feat of life could take from me. It was God-given.

The dreams in your heart matter. They matter so so much. To be sure, some dreams will fall by the wayside. Holding each one up to a filter of your values is an important step – please don't skip it. Just because I have dreams to be on stage someday, doesn't mean that I'm going to be Beyoncé. Your dreams must not only serve you, but also serve others. Oftentimes, this practically looks like just pursuing what's in your heart and as your soul begins to light on fire, there will be a natural outpouring toward others. Life begets life and it's contagious. Consider the world where dreams don't exist. Everything you consume everyday was someone's dream at one point. Chasing after, or simply allowing space for dreams to grow in your heart will ultimately move you toward the woman that you want to become. This is the way toward purpose! Permission to dream, both inside and outside, of motherhood is granted and deserved. Don't let 18-20 years go by without honoring what's inside of you, in addition to the people around you. You don't have to seek stages or publishing deals or fame by any means, but you do have to honor what's been gifted inside of you. I know we want that for our kids, so let's start with honoring it for ourselves. Make space to become a dreamer again and see where it leads you. I'm cheering you on, and showing you that I'll go first

CHAPTER 24

Secrets of Motherhood – Outsource It

I hate being the new person in a room or a crowd. It seems as though every time I show up as the new person, there usually are an entire set of unspoken social norms and underground "rules" that everyone seems to just know. And as the new girl, you're not in the know. I'm stuck looking like an idiot wondering where the manual is to fit in with this crew because no one is talking about anything specific, yet everyone seems to just *know*. This has been motherhood for me.

There are no shortcuts on how to get to the finish line of raising our kids sooner, but I do think there are life hacks that women are doing that they just aren't talking about. And as I frequently struggle day in and day out in the loneliness of being home with little's and not interacting with other adults, the more my ear begins to become attune to whispers of these secrets from other moms, of tips and tricks that were helping them along in the process. Karen has some secrets she's not sharing with you. Your goal is to get Karen talking and uncover her dirty little secrets to how she became a Karen.[12] After a couple of years of lingering on the outside circles at the playground long enough, I got close enough to the underground inner-workings of some veteran moms to discover that one of their biggest secrets to mothering is outsourcing it.

Good Lord, don't get me started on the amount of pressures and responsibilities on women in the home today. This is obnoxious and something I regularly want to punch in the face. I remember one of my first mom-friends in my early years of momming was a season ahead of me (*which, PS, HIGHLY recommend you find that woman – she will be INVALUABLE to your walk through motherhood...even if just for a season*). Her youngest child was the same age as my oldest. So she was done with the front of pretending like she had control of her household and was teaching me ALL THE THINGS.

------

[12] Karen is a fictious person we all know, and don't know, all at the same time. All likeness to your real life mom Karen is purely coincidental. □

I jumped into my role as head of our household, child-rearing professional, with absolutely NO CLUE what the hell I was doing. And also with a magical list of cosmic expectations of all the things I should be expected to accomplish during any given day. I started out real strong. Lists everywhere, reading all the parenting books – I was going to rock this thing. Until I got in it and quickly had a dose of reality: this is NO JOKE. Colicky baby? NO JOKE. Working from home while baby naps? NO JOKE. Learning how not to snap at your spouse in the middle of a sleep deprived night? NO JOKE. Sleep training, homemade baby food, discipline, figuring out which preschool to go to, registering for Kindergarten – all of it is NO JOKE. Having multiple kids in sports activities? NO JOKE. It is all just too much sometimes. The solution? We have GOT to outsource it.

For some reason there seems to be shame around outsourcing things though. We find we are ashamed to admit that we need help or that we can afford to outsource it, or that we want to work toward being able to afford outsourcing some things. Sister, there is no shame in any of that. My strengths and what I can accomplish in a day, look completely different than your strengths and what you can accomplish in a day. We can't look to the left and right to determine how to live our life. If something is overwhelming to you, yet still needs to get done, then good Lord, ask for help. Outsource it. Or better yet, let it go. There is nowhere in the manual that says you have to do all of the things *yourself.* This includes putting your kids to bed on a nightly basis. They will survive if you ask a high school neighbor girl to come put them to bed *(dare I say, they'll even be better for it?)*. This also includes and is not limited to: shopping, groceries, meal planning, house cleaning, field trips, carpool pick up and drop off – there is nowhere that says *you* must be at all of the places, and do all of the things. It is so important to really analyze your inventory and assess what you can let go of. Even if it's only on occasion, from time to time, or for a season.

There was many a day early in my motherhood journey, where after the loss of my fulltime income, we had to make some strict changes to our budget and could not afford certain things. It led us to selling our house and downsizing. Weeklong vacations morphed into weeklong trips to Mom & Dad's house in Arizona. Only getting new clothes for the kids at consignment stores instead of brand new at the box department store I used to frequent. But there were certain things that I would have sold my left arm for, before I them gave up. Mental health *(which is basically what I call babysitters)* was a non-negotiable. I had to have a babysitter if not for my marriage, at least for me. And yes, that is a paid babysitter. If you have family nearby that is willing to offer their services for free, JUMP ON IT, but we were not really in that scenario so it did hurt a lot those first few times when we had to pay actual dollar bills to someone for watching our children, but I would pay every dollar all over again because it saved my soul most days.

I also learned to let go of the pressure to be super super productive during those precious babysitter hours. Sometimes, she would show up, I'd high-five her and run as fast as I could upstairs and lock my door to crawl into bed. Friday Night Lights marathon never looked so good. Or how many times would I hop in the car, only to find myself at Target, sitting in the parking lot reading or scrolling on my phone? Not a good use of money? Maybe. But it was giving me space to be quiet and rest, and if that's what I needed for the day, then I wasn't afraid to admit it and ask for it.

Your spouse, family, or community will never know what your needs are unless you speak up and ask for help. There is no shame in outsourcing. If you can't afford certain things to be outsourced, put a flag in the ground and work toward it. If you want and need something bad enough, which I would argue that letting go of things fits that category, then you will find a way to make it work. This includes paid babysitters, this includes date nights, this includes a house cleaner – any of the things that you dream of, or know, would help make your load just a little bit lighter. As you're scrolling through Instagram, and oodling over pictures of Karen, what she isn't telling you is that she really doesn't do it all. But I'm telling you she for sure doesn't. She doesn't have perfectly curated pictures, and clean house, styled children, clean hair, *and* healthy meals prepped 4,000 times a day. And if she does, maybe consider unfollowing her – I think she's actually a bot. ⫽People don't talk about this often. And they certainly don't give permission to one another, and that needs to stop. Yes, this perspective is very much a product of white privilege which I fully recognize. Other cultures are much more communally structured and focused, so their outsourcing looks different, but it is still there, promise. The village concept is tried and true, and not invented by Americans, I can promise you that.

Look, we all have the same amount of hours in the day. The tasks of life just sometimes have to get done; I get it. Maybe you just need to get outside and go run for a bit while the babysitter is at your house. Or maybe you are just as terrible as I am in the kitchen, and you need to budget in meal swaps or cook days with your friends so that in theory, someone else is cooking for you multiple times a week. There are so many creative ways to outsource various responsibilities of motherhood, but it starts with talking about it and then asking for help. One of the secrets of motherhood though is figuring out ways to lessen your load along the way, despite the number of kids that you have, in order to be ready to step into the real game when the time comes. I want to be present for my kids when they get off the bus (*some days*). I want to have earned that right to be heard from them early on, and for me, that meant investing in my mental health on an ongoing basis, otherwise there's no way I could show up as a whole healthy person. When it's game time, I want to have the energy and capacity to say yes to the responsibility of child-rearing and guiding their hearts – this means freeing up some emotional capacity from another area. Something will have to give one thousand percent. The daily tasks that are required to run a household will absolutely suck the life out of you, and leave you feeling overwhelmed and inadequate if you don't assess, analyze, and start outsourcing at least something. You can't do it all. So make space and room to at least do the most important things. Your kids, marriage, and friends will thank you later. ▯

CHAPTER 25

Just Start Somewhere

"Be fearless in the pursuit of what sets your soul on fire."

-Rachel Hollis

We are all searching for purpose and significance. That is probably one of the main reasons why you picked up this book *(unless you're my mom, then you probably bought it because that's just what moms do – they support their kiddos)*. You were drawn in with the question of wanting to know your purpose in life and were hoping for some answers. This is a universal desire deep from within. I believe that each culture and society defines these things differently, but in Western culture oftentimes purpose and significance is associated with vocation and success. To achieve success as a mom feels like trying to find a four-leaf clover in the deserts of Egypt, when you use those standards as the measuring stick.

For me, it has helped so much to write out my journey. I have needed to see how far I have come. And that I'm still standing. I have needed to see the intentionality that I *have* poured into and invested in with my marriage, my friends, and my community. These are not in vain. That voice telling you that you are not enough is a lie. And oftentimes in order to see the lie for what it is, you need to take a step back and just celebrate and reflect on how far you've come.

And if you begin that journey, and you take a step back and you don't like what you see – you feel like there's too many mess ups, you haven't been your best self and you can only see the negatives of how you've chosen to use your time; then GRACE. Today's a new day. You're reading this book which tells me that you DO care, that you do want purpose and that you want your life and role as a mom to mean something. You are doing better than you think and a simple mindset shift will help you begin to believe it deep in your core.

When I finally began to get my head above water, I realized that this magical idea of purpose wasn't just going to fall into my lap. That I was going to need to put myself out there and just start somewhere. Literally the only thing I knew was that I wanted more. I didn't know the how, I didn't know the when, I just knew I had a tiny spark within and I wanted to fan it into a flame.

First thing I did, was dust off the ole resume document on my computer *(which literally hadn't been opened or updated in way too many years)* and began applying and interviewing. My first interview after being out of the formal working world for eight years was at a local smoothie shop.

Let that just sink in for a minute. Smoothie. Shop.

Dude, I know – what the hell was I thinking?!

It's not the one that you're all thinking of, but it basically was that. And I thought that if I could just do something mindless, something to get me away from the kids for just a few hours, that that would bring me happiness and contentment. I walked into the smoothie shop and just laughed. It was a serious reality check. I heard the constant blare and noise of the blenders. I saw the constant washing of the dishes, and I thought "what am I doing here?" I was at a smoothie shop! This is a glorified version of the crap I'm already doing at home! And not that I am *above* doing this type of work as a vocation, but this was a goofy farse of an escape. I actually have several friends who have wonderful 'mom jobs' as they call them – fun retail work where they do actually get to lean into their giftings for hospitality and helpfulness that these roles offer. I'm not against this avenue at all. I just knew that it wasn't a pursuit that would be leaning into *my* unique giftings and purpose, and I was trying to take the easy way out. I was running from what was hard, and the hard was at home. I wanted that Staples Easy Button again.

Stop running from the unknown. Stop **searching** for the magical solution to your feelings of discontent. Your greatest gift and life's work most likely is just right under your nose. Some people do need to take a drastic left turn and start working at the smoothie shop. But my hunch is that most of us have something right in front of us already, that we're doing our best to try to avoid. For me, it was my kids and my marriage. The main door that had been opened for me was to love on my family. I already had the freedom and flexibility to make an impact in my community. I had the chops to influence and lead (*albeit on a seriously small scale*), and I needed to stop disqualifying myself from the biggest job I had ever been blessed with: being a mom.

Even though domestic prowess wasn't my specialty, there were other things that I possessed that could serve the people right under my nose well. I wish I could say I had all of the answers, but the reality is that my kids are still super YOUNG and I still don't know what I'm doing. But I'm tired of dodging it. I'm tired of discounting it. This is the job I prayed for, and have been given. It is freaking hard. I hate it some days, I love it others, and I cry a lot. And most days, I have NO CLUE what I'm doing. But I'm choosing to lean in now instead of escape or run.

The solution to finding your purpose, and ultimately feeling more purposeful, is most likely not to ADD more to your plate. The solution to finding your purpose is simply to start right where you're at, and take one step forward with your current everyday life. Little kids? Lean in. Caring for an ailing parent? Lean in. Trust that your story is not over. This is not the end of your road. There may be a career ahead of you, with paychecks and titles, promotions and co-workers that don't talk back, and there may not. Either way, your goals, your purpose, your life's work, starts now. Motherhood is an investment oftentimes in something that we can't even see. Our job is to water the plants, not make them grow. Sometimes our investments will grow, and some won't. We don't have to worry about that though, because our job is simply keep showing up, planting and watering.

I believe that every single one of us has a unique role to play and song to sing. We are not promised tomorrow, so we need to stop living as if we are. Today is what you've been given. So if you find yourself changing diapers, and wiping snotty noses, and caring for fever-ridden little's who just need every single ounce of you, I get it; it's hard and exhausting, but you will not get to the end of your life wanting just one more day at work or the office. You will want your life to have meant something to the people that you love the most. That is the heart of our human desire. We want to mean something to someone, and particularly the someone's that we love the most. We want our efforts to feel purposeful and meaningful. You start that process by leaning in right where you're at. The chase of something greater will leave you feeling empty. Trust me, I know firsthand, I've done it for years.

EPILOGUE

(That Feels Fancier Than This Book, But They Tell Me I Should Have It)

I have chosen to make a career out of loving my family and loving my neighbors. It's not the traditional route. And frankly, it didn't even require that fun fancy college education I got (*thanks Mom & Dad!*), but I have finally come to see and believe that there is so much value in this work. Trust me, when you look at my skillset on paper, it doesn't make much sense that my career would be loving the people in my home fulltime. I am NOT Martha Stewart; I don't know my way around the kitchen AT ALL. I am not precious in the slightest and stereotypically it makes zero sense when you look at my gifts and try to match it with what a full time stay at home mom is responsible for. But stereotype or not, this is the path that I am on. It may not be the path that I'm on next year, or in 5 years, but it's where I'm at right now. And accepting my current reality was the first step toward feeling purposeful.

We can have ripple effects for generations just by loving the people placed right in front of us. This is our call, and this is our job. We are to love well, love recklessly; everyone, always. There will be no greater call or purpose for our life. Sure, there will be other vocations and opportunities that get placed on our path, and those are all great and good, but I don't want to miss the point anymore. My job or a paycheck will not be the thing that brings me purpose. If I have to choose to exchange my time and my life for anything, I choose my family all day long. We all do, I know it. On our death bed, if we can look back and see a life well-loved, then I have a feeling we will render all of the long and hard days as worth it. Even the ones with vomit and butt-wiping.

You are worth it. And you are doing better than you think, right where you're at. You are equipped to live out whatever purpose you have been put on this Earth to accomplish. And nothing that you ever accomplish will be the thing that fills you. That is not the end goal. We are to love, and be loved. That is the gift of life. I have not always believed these things, and man oh man, motherhood has challenged these beliefs in me more than anything else in life. But my hope is that by sharing my journey, my every day, run of the mill regular life, that you will see the still-small progress of beauty that you are creating just by showing up in your regular, run of the mill, everyday life. By using what you have, right where you're at. How that's ultimately helping craft a beautiful legacy and existence one poopy diaper, one snotty nose, one timeout, one preschool drop-off, one Chuck E. Cheese birthday party, at a time.

It's going to be work though ladies. I mean for real, we're going to need to gird our loins (*I literally have never known what that means*). I am a firm believer that yes, we are loved as is, but we are not called to stay that way. And oftentimes, it means we need to pull ourselves, and our sisters, up by the bootstraps because this journey of motherhood is no freaking joke. Raising kids in the social media generation is no joke. Walking the tension of female empowerment and traditional gender roles within the nuclear family as modern women is no joke. We will be a generation of moms that lives fully into holding grace and power at the same time. We've been raised to believe that we can do it all and even though the sentiment of that message is empowering and confidence-building (*something we do want to pass on to our sons and daughters*), it is not true. We can't do it all. And that is so okay because we don't need to. Loving our people absolutely imperfectly and wholly is all that will ever be needed or required for a purposeful life. That's it, sister. The cliff notes for the entire book and the recipe for the whole thing is simply to leave it all on the court. Blood, sweat, and tears and it will be enough. Because the job that you are doing is enough, because you are enough and more than a mom.

Thank You's

I have tried with all of my might to build the daily practice of gratitude into my life as a means to feel purposeful and content. Writing this book is no exception and it took a whole freaking village to get here.

First and foremost, I want to thank my kids. Without whom, there would be approximately zero content for this book. To my boys, I *always* envisioned myself as a boy mom and both of you bring me so much joy. Brecken, as my first-born, you were just the cutest ever. I obsessed fanatically over every word, every noise, every step you took. I loved every part about cuddling with you and my heart literally just exploded when I became your mom. You are a stud and watching you on the baseball field is literally a straight up dream come true. My sweet Brenner bear, ugh you are my favorite (don't tell the other two), but I just get you on so many levels. You have a heart of gold and I've never thought I deserved someone as pure-hearted and sweet as you. I love you so much buddy. And for Brynley, you are everything I never knew I needed. You are my dream daughter – spicy and sassy with style and spunk and fire and passion, and I just love everything about the adult that you will someday become.

To the mamas that have walked these seasons with me each step of the way. There have been different groups of you, depending on proximity, but each of you have helped me raise me (while also raising these kids). Danielle, Hillary, Kendra, Amanda – you taught me how to be a mom. Made me laugh, listened to me cry, and continued to point me forward. We were in the trenches together and I'm forever grateful for our friendships during that season.

To Kendra, I would be everywhere and nowhere without you. Good thing we have unlimited texting at this point, because I've probably talked to you more over the last 10 years than I have to my husband. You're my middle of the night, my Dateline alibi, my one call from jail, my plus one, and forever my partner in crime. The growth that we each have experienced is something that can't ever be taken away – we became who we are today with each other and I just don't have another friend in my life like you.

To Whitney, Lauren, and Britt – you guys are my forevers. My truth tellers, my soul sisters, the ones that I can always count on to pray over me, point me back to truth and encourage me through the seasons. I am SO grateful that our friendships have existed outside of, and before motherhood, but it is a dream that we all get to carry on second-generation friends with our kids now as we walk the road of motherhood together. We don't need to live in the same city for me to know that I can spend an hour with you and it'll be like no time has passed. I love you forever.

To my Bossy Mamas. I've never loved the name of our group, but I love me some small business mamas. You each have pushed and cheered me on during the final laps of this journey, inspired me to dig deeper in me to uncover and finesse what it's taken to bring this out into the world, and held me accountable along the way. Thankful to have bosses like you in my corner of the ring because you each have shown me there is more in me than I would have ever given myself credit for.

To my family of origin – Ames, Mom, & Dad. You have loved me, shaped me, and walked with me literally through everything. I am grateful for the work Mom and Dad put in to me as a stubborn first-born kid needing to find her own way. And Ames, as my one and only sister, there is no one else in my life but you. My forever best friend. What a joy it is to get to mom together now as we navigate raising these kids as cousins, and sisters. I love you all.

To the slough of babysitters who have watched my children for countless hours offering me bits and pieces of sanity over the years. You've seen me at my worst, and best, and still have come back to love on and care for our kids as if they were your own. You each have been my LIFELINE in various seasons. Brooklyn, Lindsay, Miss Micailah & Miss Elizabeth, and every other random girl with a pulse in our neighborhoods – this book doesn't exist without you 1000%.

To my neighbor girls. I call you my neighbor girls just for category purposes but you are no less my friend than anyone else. Sometimes it's crazy for me to think that you haven't been in my life longer than the past 3.5 years, but I'm so so grateful. You accepted my un-fancy ways and circled up around living the free-range everyday life in this dreamy 'hood of ours that I always envisioned. Grateful to have found each of you in this latest chapter of life and am grateful for all of our impromptu Crappy Dinner Parties, wine nights, beach hangs, and low-bar lifestyle that we each live out and promote. You are all so my people and my dream friends.

To my editor + proofreader extraordinaire Rachael Mitchell – thanks for taking a chance on me. Can't wait to ride this all the way to the top knowing we did this thing with grass roots effort, mixed in with a lot of grit and determination. When all of the literary agents and basically anyone else with a fancy publishing pedigree said no, you were my yes. Thankful to have met you and your skillset to polish this baby off. Thanks for being my first co-worker that doesn't talk back since taking on the title of Mom.

To the leaders who spoke life into me and called out things in me that I didn't believe for myself. Jamie Lisea – you gave me a seat at the table in a season where I didn't feel like I deserved it. And from that, I was able to finally take my blinders off and step into the woman who I know God created me to be. So so grateful for your encouragement to me and willingness to always include me in the conversation, even when it looks on paper like I have no business being there. Jeremy Johnson – I will never forget your leadership to me in a season of being a new mom, constantly calling out and encouraging character traits in me that propelled me forward. Our friendship with you and Leanne is forever one of our faves. Ashley Grau – even though we never mommed together, you took me under your wing and taught me to go after everything I could want. You led me and released me to lead others in such a powerful way. We could've run the world; I'm convinced of it. To Jodie McClure, who took the time to invest in a scrawny fourteen-year-old who was brattier than she was fun. I am forever grateful to you for introducing me to Jesus as the friend that I had never met.

To the women who mentored me and didn't even know it. Jen Hatmaker, you have been my pastor and wordsmith North Star for YEARS, when I was wandering and had nowhere faith-wise to land that was safe. You've publicly laid a path for me that allows me to see a future road I too can walk as my full self and still love Jesus. Melissa Radke, Rachel Hollis, Jennie Allen – your words and work have encouraged me and helped me uncover the fire and passion within just by being faithful to what you have been called to do. I hope someday I can do the same for someone else.

And finally, to Blake. I cry just typing your name. You are my best friend and we had no freaking clue in hell what we were doing when we started this (*and still don't*). You have chosen to love me through every iteration of me. I know it hasn't been easy, but we've walked this road together and this is the life we created and built, and no one else has the same perspective on it as you. Our marriage has been the bright spot for me for so many years and the one thing that I always knew I could lean on. I know it's gotten hairy as we've had to re-establish what normal looks like for us as I've began working again and ploughing forward into this new path, but I'm so so grateful you've still chosen to stick it out. I know that you support me through it all, even when I'm riding the latest crazy train (*blame the kids*). We were just two kids without a dime to our name, dreaming up the power couple days that we would someday claim as our own. Ha! I wouldn't trade our current reality for anything else. We're living the dream. Thank you for loving me through every re-birth of myself that I've gone through over the past 16 years.

Book Club Questions (Dear Oprah & Reese, I Wrote These For You)

Chapter 1: Four Letter Words

- How do you typically respond when someone asks you what you do? Especially if you are a stay-at-home-mom, what is the language you use to describe that job?
- In what ways has motherhood been easy for you?
- In what ways has motherhood been hard for you?

Chapter 2: Surviving Not Thriving

- What do you feel when you hear the phrase thriving not surviving?
- In your current phase, which would you describe is more fitting of where you're at: surviving not thriving, or thriving not surviving?
- What was it like for you the first time you took a positive pregnancy test? What were the circumstances surrounding it?

Chapter 3: Never-Ending Seasons

- What has been the hardest season of motherhood so far for you? Why?
- Take some time to survey what seasons you have moved out of, and what season you are in. Sometimes in order to feel accomplished, it takes us surveying just how far we've come. Write it down. Look through the baby book (you may or may not have made), scroll old pictures on your phone. Give yourself the gift of perspective to see how far you've come to better adjust the story you are telling yourself about where your identity is rooted.
- When was a time that you felt embarrassed because of your kids' behavior?
- How does it make you feel to hear, and accept, that your value and worth are not tied to your kids' accomplishments or failures? Do you already believe this about yourself, or is this a new concept?

Chapter 4: The Career Ship Sails

- What was the transition like for you when you became a mom?
- What was the biggest thing you had to give up from your previous life?
- What has been the biggest surprise of something you've gained since becoming a mom?
- When is a time that you have made plans for your future, only to get there and realize you needed a different map?

Chapter 5: One More Lonely Girl

- How do you experience loneliness in the everyday as a mom?
- What are some of the losses that you've experienced since becoming a mom?
- Is there any part of your life right now that you feel like you are grieving?

Chapter 6: Secret Society Of Anxiety Meds

- What has been your experience with post-partum depression? Both with yourself and your social circles?
- Who are the people you'd say you have in your life that you safely reveal the last 10% to?

Chapter 7: Unfit For The Mold

- Take inventory of you. Start by making a list of things on your plate. Make two different columns – one of things that won't change (i.e. being a mom, being a wife, etc.) along with additional responsibilities that can easily change (i.e. MOPS leader, PTA participant, business owner, etc.). Identify to someone out loud which of these sucks the life out of you, and which brings you life.
- What is a current responsibility or role that you can quit?
- When is it that you feel most like you?

Chapter 8: Wheel Of Worthiness

- What is one secret hobby/bucket list goal you have for yourself (note: it must be outside of motherhood)?

- If you were to be gifted an extra $5,000 today, how would you choose to use that money? What would be the one thing that you'd do for yourself with it?

Chapter 9: Stay In Your Lane

- What is your belief on the notion that simply being a mom – without any other formal vocation on your resume – is enough?
- Have you ever asked your people what they think you're really good at? What were the results? What were the repeating patterns?
- Where is it in life that you most come alive, that you feel most integrated as your full self?
- What is the dream in your heart, outside of motherhood?

Chapter 10: It Doesn't Add Up

- What are the areas of your life that you feel least qualified for?
- Similar to the little boy in the story, what is the "little" that you can offer from your everyday life?

Chapter 11: Laugh More, Laugh Often

- Who are you with when you most frequently get the giggles?
- What is one regular rhythm of fun that you can incorporate into your normal schedule?
- When is the last time that you laughed until your cheeks hurt the next day?

Chapter 12: Parenting In The Trenches

- On a scale from one to lonely, how satisfied are you with your current friend situation?
- When was the last time that you made a new friend?
- What is one way that you could invite, or include, someone new into your circle of friends (if you have one)?

Chapter 13: Unsolicited Advice

- How has unsolicited advice from others harmed, or caused doubt, in your parenting?
- Dream up scenarios for each of your kids as a way to spend one on one time with them. Doesn't need to be extravagant, just has to happen. Tell a friend or partner your plans.
- What would it look like for you to cheer on someone else's victories in parenting, even if you don't agree with them?

Chapter 14: The Easy Button

- What was your dream job when you were growing up as a kid? How has it differed over the years?
- How is your role right now as a mom different, or the same, as what you envisioned?

Chapter 15: Open Doors

- What are the things that you can most easily spend your money on? Hint: look at your bank account.
- What does financial generosity look like for you in this season of life?

Chapter 16: Find Your People

- What does it look for you to engage in everyday rest right now?
- Do you feel like you have a go-to person in motherhood?
- How has having your person impacted your job as a mom? What about if you don't have that person (sister wife) – how has that impacted your job as a mom?

Chapter 17: Dressing For The Job

- In what ways do you incorporate self-care into your wardrobe?
- When you look at yourself in the mirror naked, what do you see?
- What do you for soul care? How are self-care and soul care different in your opinion?

Chapter 18: The Grass Is Greener Where You Water It

- What are your go-to methods to zone out or escape when the monotony starts to get to you?
- How have you seen the "grass is greener where you water it" principle play out in your life?

Chapter 19: Live With Intention

- What are some key patterns that you have been able to identify about yourself throughout your life? (Examples would be: leading, helping, building, giving, serving, planning, inviting)
- Identify some of the key pillars that you want for your life in terms of legacy. What are they, and how will you go about working toward them?

- How can you live with more intention in your everyday life?

Chapter 20: Heart Work Is Hard Work (The Sex Chapter)

- How would you rate your sex life right now with your partner?
- Do you regularly talk about sex with your partner, or is it something that doesn't really get discussed often?
- How has motherhood effected, or changed, your sex life?

Chapter 21: No Bailouts

- How do you disintguish your efforts as a mom with your kids' behavior/choices?
- How would you have handled the Forgotten Book Fair Money situation in your family?

Chapter 22: People Matter, Invite Them Over

- What is something that you already love to do, and are good at doing?
- What role do friends play in your life?
- How do you currently celebrate others?

Chapter 23: Becoming A Dreamer Again

- What are the dreams in your heart?
- What are the visions or thoughts that you've seen in the quiet moments of your heart?
- Who would your twenty-one-year-old self think your 35-year-old self would be doing?

- Is there a dream you've let go because of motherhood? Or have you let it go because it seemed like it wouldn't work anymore?
- How will the world be without your dream in it?
- When you anticipate dreaming, what are you afraid of?

Chapter 24: Secrets Of Motherhood – Outsource It

- What is currently on your plate that you can quit, outsource, or let go of?
- How do you feel about asking for help? When was the last time that you asked someone for help on the regular?

Chapter 25: Just Start Somewhere

- What do you want your life to mean someday?
- How do you want your kids to describe you when they leave your care? Is that person who you are today, or someone you're striving toward?
- What is your next step toward feeling more purposeful?

List of Resources

I am not afraid to acknowledge that MANY people have gone before me, shared their stories, which have thus influenced and inspired me along the way. This is by no means an exhaustive list, but it is definitely the one that is most top of mind of resources for you to devour, many of which were referenced in this book. My hope is this becomes a starting road map if you will to seek out and hopefully in turn do the work to find peace and grace within yourself to feel significantly purposeful in how you live out your days.

Books:

Allen, Jennie. *Proven: Where Christ's Abundance Meets Our Great Need.* Tennesse: LifeWay Press, 2017.

Allen, Jennie. *Restless: Because You Were Made For More.* Tennessee: Thomas Nelson, 2014.

Brown, Brené. *Daring Greatly: How the Courage To Be Vulnerable Transforms the Way We Live, Love, Parent, and Lead.* New York: Avery, 2015.

Defeo, Courtney. *In This House We Will Giggle: Making Virtues, Love, and Laughter a Daily Part of Your Family.* Colorado: WaterBrook, 2014.

Goff, Bob. *Love Does: Discover a Secretly Incredible Life in an Ordinary World.* Tennessee: Thomas Nelson, 2012.

Goff, Maria. *Love Lives Here: Finding What You Need in a World Telling You What You Want.* Tennessee: B&H Books, 2017.

Gresham, Clint. *Becoming: Loving The Process To Wholeness.* Texas: Fortem Press, 2017.

Hatmaker, Jen. *Interrupted: When Jesus Wrecks Your Comfortable Christianity.* Illinois: Navpress, 2014.

Hatmaker, Jen. *Of Mess and Moxie: Wrangling Delight Out of This Wild and Glorious Life.* Tennessee: Thomas Nelson, 2017.

Hollis, Rachel. *Girl, Wash Your Face: Stop Believing the Lies About Who You Are So You Can Becomes Who You Were Meant to Be.* Tennessee: Thomas Nelson, 2018.

Honegger, Jessica. *Imperfect Courage: Live a Life of Purpose by Leaving Comfort and Going Scared.* New York: WaterBrook, 2018.

Huertz, Chris. *Sacred Enneagram: Finding Your Unique Path to Spiritual Growth.* Michigan: Zondervan, 2017.

Lentz, Carl. *Own The Moment.* New York: Simon & Schuster, 2017.

Moore, Beth. *Breaking Free: The Journey, The Stories.* Tennessee: LifeWay Press, 2009.

Olthoff, Bianca. *Play With Fire: Discovering Fierce Faith, Unquenchable Passion, and a Life-Giving God.* Michigan: Zondervan, 2016.

Peterson, Michelle. *#staymarried: A Couple's Devotional.* Texas: Althea Press, 2017.

Radke, Melissa. *Eat Cake. Be Brave.* New York: Grand Central Publishing, 2018.

Podcasts:

The Rise Podcast by Rachel Hollis

Next Right Thing by Emily P. Freeman

Risen Motherhood by Ashlee Gadd

God-Centered Mom by Heather McFaydden

How I Built This by Guy Richards

That Sounds Fun by Annie F. Downs

The Road Back To You by Ian Crohn & Suzanne Stabile

#staymarried Podcast by Michelle & Tony Peterson

---

[i] Move the Cheese book

[ii] Brene Brown comparitive suffering

16358613R00164